Scope

Handbook 2

Pronunciation : for Immigrant Children from India, Pakistan, Cyprus and Italy

Elizabeth Rudd
Schools Council Project
in English for
Immigrant Children

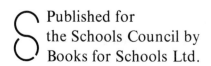
Published for
the Schools Council by
Books for Schools Ltd.

Books for Schools Ltd. London

© Schools Council Publications 1971

First published 1971
ISBN 0 582 09026 1

All the materials arising from the Schools
Council Project in English for Immigrant
Children are published for the Schools
Council by Books for Schools Ltd., a
consortium of the following publishers:

Councils and Education Press Ltd.
Ginn & Company Ltd.
Longman Group Ltd.
Newnes Educational Publishing Company Ltd.
Oliver & Boyd Ltd.
The Schoolmaster Publishing Company Ltd.

The Longman Group Ltd., who are
responsible for the production of the
materials, are the distributors on behalf
of Books for Schools Ltd., and all
general enquiries should be sent to them
at Longman House, Burnt Mill, Harlow, Essex.

Photoset and printed in Malta
by St Paul's Press Ltd.

Scope

Handbook 2

Pronunciation : for
Immigrant Children
from India, Pakistan,
Cyprus and Italy

Scope

Scope An introductory
English course for
immigrant children
Stage 1

Teacher's package

Teacher's book

Pupils' books:
Picture book
Work book
Readers 1–8

Scope Handbooks
for teachers

Handbook 1
The social background
of Immigrant Children
from India, Pakistan
and Cyprus

Handbook 2
Pronunciation : for
Immigrant Children
from India, Pakistan,
Cyprus and Italy

These materials were
prepared by the
Schools Council Project
in English for Immigrant
Children at the
Institute of Education
Leeds University

Contents

Preface

In writing this book, I am particularly indebted to the following people for their time and advice: Miss June Derrick, Mr. K. Lodge, Mr. P. A. D. MacCarthy, Mr. A. E. Smith and Mr. J. W. Spencer, all of the University of Leeds, and Mr. M. Vodden of the British Council. Furthermore, without the help and experience of a large number of teachers associated formally or informally with the Project, the book would not have been possible at all.

Acknowledgements

We are grateful to the following for permission to reproduce copyright material:

Mrs. Joan Bennett for 'This and That' and 'Water in Bottles' by Rodney Bennett; A. & C. Black Limited for 'The Spider' by Winifred Kingdon-Ward from *A Book of Rhymes and Jingles* and 'The Farmyard' by Clive Sansom from *Speech Rhymes*; Curtis Brown Limited and E. P. Dutton & Company Inc. for 'The Four Friends' from *When We Were Very Young* by A. A. Milne. Copyright, 1924, by E. P. Dutton & Co. Inc. Renewal, 1952, by A. A. Milne; George G. Harrap & Company Limited for 'Here Comes a Big Red Bus' and 'Heads and Shoulders' from *Music for the Nursery School* by Linda Chesterman; Oxford University Press for 'Where is my Pencil' from *Argonauts' English Course* by W. R. Lee and L. Koullis; Sir Isaac Pitman & Sons Limited for 'What Are You Going To Be' from *Songs and Marching Tunes for Children.*

We have been unable to trace the copyright holder of 'Clocks' and would appreciate any information that would enable us to do so.

PART ONE

1 Introduction

When do you *live*?
What?
?

---

1   Intelligibility

This book is concerned with the speech of immigrant
children whose English is not easy to understand since it is not
their native language. You, as the child's teacher, are in the
best position to tackle the problems involved, and in this
book we have suggested detailed objectives, teaching techniques and practice material. You will be able to use the book
whether or not you have any background in phonetics or
linguistics.

Many people believe that a learner can pick up an adequate
pronunciation on his own, and that a teacher need not
concern himself with this side of language teaching.
Unfortunately there is no justification for this view. Only
a child who starts very young or spends all his time with native
speakers can hope to manage without special help. Speech
habits, once established, tend to remain.

The greatest communication problems will arise when the
child wants to talk to someone new, especially if the person
is not practised in listening to English spoken by foreigners.
People with the child constantly – his teacher for example –
become used to his speech and, because they know him
very well, are able to guess the bits they might not otherwise
have followed. Here, comprehension depends on the listener's
familiarity with the immigrant child, his community and
situation. Many of the people the child will want to speak to,
however, will not have this familiarity, and they will find it
very difficult to understand him. At the same time, the child
will expect everyone to understand him as easily as his teacher
does.

One's aims must be realistic. Few immigrants are likely to
become so bilingual that their pronunciation is indistinguish-
able from that of native speakers; but this does not matter
very much. The important thing is that they should be easily
understood by people whose ears are not specially attuned.

3

They must be able to communicate effectively with everyone. They may always sound like Indians, Pakistanis, Cypriots, Italians; but then, we are already used to different accents among ourselves. Moreover, educated speakers from different parts of Britain and from other English-speaking countries sound very different but can still understand each other well. Nevertheless, the learner of a new language is fumbling for an accent that he can produce easily and that other people can follow easily, and right from the beginning he needs help. We must help him to listen carefully and to imitate native speakers; we must identify the features that make him hard to understand and help him to lose them. Sometimes one finds that these features seem insignificant when considered one by one and that loss of understanding results from their quantity and variety rather than from their individual nature. The speaker of a second language has other difficulties besides pronunciation, and these will also hinder understanding. Consequently it is all the more important that what he actually says should be said clearly. The listener must make an effort to understand a speaker with an unfamiliar accent, but the less effort demanded, the better for both listener and speaker.

If you are in constant contact with a child, you may not find it easy to judge his pronunciation. You may feel that it has become clearer; but has it? It may be simply that your ears are becoming more attuned to his speech. The tape recorder is one effective means of judging speech improvement over a period of time, because it enables you to listen to one sample of speech more than once and to compare it with earlier samples. Another useful indicator is the visitor to the class, especially one who is not used to listening to immigrant children or foreigners. Which children can he understand easily? Which ones can he not understand at all? Let some of the children act out a dialogue for him. How much of the speech can he understand? Can he make out what is happening at all? Explain to him why you want his honest reactions, or he may be reluctant to admit that he cannot understand.

When thinking about intelligibility, ask yourself whether 'the man in the street' could understand the child easily. Think of listeners in less than ideal listening situations and who are not used to hearing foreigners. Imagine an immigrant teenager being interviewed for a job which he wants very badly; the excitement and urgency of the situation will not

4

help him to speak more clearly. The busy interviewer is perhaps not very imaginative or patient. If the immigrant's speech seems indistinct and he is difficult to understand, he may not get that job. It would be interesting to have more detailed information about the effect of difficult speech on inter-racial relationships in factories, other work places and social situations, and in transient encounters in buses, restaurants, shops and so on.

Regional variations in accent raise another question, especially if you come from one region and teach in another. What kind of accent should you teach? In fact, you are bound to teach the accent you have yourself, and provided you are a native speaker, any accent will do. If you have one accent and the local British children have another, you will probably find your immigrant children speak more and more like the other children as time goes on, and this must be all to the good, since it will help them to feel part of the local community. If you are not a native speaker, it is very important to enlist the help of someone who is, and preferably who knows you well enough to feel able to tell you about any special pronunciation peculiarities you have which the children will imitate, and who will possibly let you tape his voice for use in class and even give the occasional lesson.

What does pronunciation teaching involve? How does one really know if a child is 'intelligible' or not? Can one say, in any definitive sense, that this child is intelligible and that one is not? Let us put the question rather differently, assume that maximum intelligibility is desirable and ask what features of a child's speech are obstructing this. Initially, we can map out certain problem areas:

1. Speech rhythm and stress Do important words and syllables stand out when the child speaks, or does he give equal weight and time to each syllable, so that the general effect is either extremely monotonous or else very gabbled?

2. Individual speech sounds Is the child producing any of these in a way that prevents us from recognising easily the words he is using? For example, can we tell the difference between minimally different words like *live* and *leave* or *bill* and *pill*?

3. Intonation Listen to the melodic shape or tune of his speech. Does he vary his voice pitch at all, and if so, is it in a way that makes him easier and more interesting to listen to?

4. Confidence and fluency How would you rate him for these? Is he always hesitant or does he speak confidently sometimes? If so, when is he confident and when is he not? Is he eager to talk or reluctant to do so?

We can be sure that if a child is failing in any of these areas – and he will probably be having difficulties in all of them, even if he has been in England for several years – it will be difficult for the unspecialised ear to understand. We can work on all these problem areas, however, and area number one is by far the most important. A very large part of this book is taken up by area number two, but this reflects the variety of different problems you may meet rather than the relative amount of time you should spend on practising individual sounds. Pronunciation is as important as any other aspect of language, and it is not hard to achieve perceptible improvement. In any case, if a child cannot speak clearly enough to be understood easily, it means much of his other language ability is unusable; and after all, language is a tool for communicating. If something is preventing this, the tool is useless.

2 Learning the sounds of a new language

Your children are most likely to speak one or more of the following languages: Hindi, Urdu, Gujerati, Punjabi, Greek or Turkish if they come from Cyprus, or Italian; and much of this book focuses on the problems of learners with these as a mother tongue. In many cases they will speak dialect forms. Some children will already be bilingual. If some of your class speak other languages,[1] you will still find Part One of the book directly relevant, and many of the suggestions in Part Two will be useful once you have identified their particular pronunciation difficulties.

The differences between a native language and a second language that has to be learnt are responsible for many of the mistakes a learner makes. Anyone hearing a new sound in a new language will try to fit it into his existing experience of

---

[1]The Centre for Information on Language Teaching (C.I.L.T.) in State House, High Holborn, London W C 1 has a wide range of books, papers and information on language teaching and the problems of different groups of learners.

language sounds, and to equate it with one already familiar, probably in his native language. But the sound systems of different languages are composed and constructed very differently, and one cannot match them up in this way.

Imagine two languages; let us call them language A and language B. It is unlikely that they would have the same number of vowel sounds, and to simplify matters, let us suppose that language A has only three different vowel sounds and language B only five different ones. Note that we are considering vowel sounds, not the letters A, E, I, O, U. English has nearly twice as many sounds as letters, and few languages have a one-to-one relationship between their sound system and their spelling system. The diagram below shows how these two imaginary vowel sound systems might relate to one another. The numbers represent distinct vowel sounds. There will be similarities at some points between the two languages; and where we want to show that two vowels are virtually the same, we have placed them exactly level on the diagram, as in the case of number (1) and (4).

Language A	Language B
(1)	(4)
(2)	(5)
	(6)
(3)	(7)
	(8)

Now, imagine that a language A speaker wants to learn language B. The first sound he meets in language B is (4) and he finds this is identical with his own familiar (1); so here he has no difficulty. The next language B sound he meets is (5), and this sounds very much like his own (2), and so he thinks that he is safe here too. But then he meets sound (6) and finds that it, also, sounds like his own (2); in consequence he becomes very confused about sounds (5) and (6), mistakes them for each other, and uses his own sound (2) to serve for both when trying to speak language B; and, of course, language B speakers find him confusing because he is making different words in their language sound the same. For example, if language B had been English and vowels (5) and (6) had been the vowels in the words *live* and *leave*, the learner would have made these two words sound identical and the listener would soon have become very confused. When he meets language B sound (7) he finds that it is really very like his own sound (3). Actually they are not quite the same, but his slightly deviant pronunciation does not confuse anyone; he just sounds faintly odd. Finally, he has to learn a completely new sound, (8), for which there is no near-match in his native language; he has to start from scratch.

This is a gross simplification of the way in which one's native language experience interferes with one's pronunciation of a new language, but it does demonstrate certain factors at work. It also makes it easier to understand why sounds that seem to us so obviously different, such as s and ʃ (as in *sell* and *shell*) may sound exactly the same to some learners, and why learners from different language-speaking communities have different problems with English. The same kind of interference arises with grammar, vocabulary and the social conventions governing our use of language. Before expecting a child to make two words like *sell* and *shell* distinct, therefore, make sure he can hear the difference between them, and if he cannot, give him the opportunity to practise differentiating between them.[1] He will eventually succeed, but it takes a little time in some cases. Ear training work must be done however before improvement in production can be expected.

---

[1] For details about practice in differentiation, see pp. 30 and 36.

2 Major features –
What has to be taught

This section can do no more than point to the most
important features of the English sound system, and explain
a few basic concepts that will help you when working on
pronunciation. There are several books that deal simply but
far more comprehensively with this subject, and you would
be well advised to go on to read these.[1]

1 Component sounds

The learner is faced with a new inventory of sounds, which
he must learn to recognise in the rapid speech of native
speakers and to use himself. As indicated above, some of
these sounds will already be familiar, some will not but
can be imitated easily. He may find it hard to distinguish
some, and others may seem to him so like his native language
sounds that he will use those instead, not realising that to
English ears there is a difference. The result may then be
simply a foreign flavour to his English, or it may be completely
baffling to the English listener. Some of these difficulties will
be troublesome for a while, but soon overcome. Some are
likely to persist unless given careful attention. Furthermore,
mastering component sounds is only an early step in the
process of mastering speech in a second language. Combining
them, evenly and with correct stress and intonation is even
more important; and in due course the learner will come to
learn how to project his own subtleties of feeling and attitude
in the new language.

---

[1] P. MacCarthy, *English Pronunciation*, Heffer. Julian T. Pring, *Colloquial
English Pronunciation*, Longman. J. D. O'Connor, *Better English Pronunciation*,
Cambridge University Press. Daniel Jones, *The Pronunciation of English*,
Heffer, 1964 (revised).

The sound system of a language must not be confused with its alphabet and spelling system. Letters relate to sounds, but the two never amount to the same thing. In some languages there is a very simple and direct relationship between spelling and pronunciation; every letter in the written word corresponds to a sound in the spoken word; but this is not so with English; it has twenty-six letters and nearly twice as many sounds; and the relationship between the two, it need hardly be said, is very complex. Therefore it is very dangerous to refer to sounds by the names of letters when teaching pronunciation. The two must be kept distinct; and this book is concerned with sounds and pronunciation, not with their relationship to spelling and reading. For this reason, it is unwise to give written material to the class as a basis for pronunciation work, for the learner will be misled by the spelling – especially if his native language is one where words are pronounced as they are spelt. It is also one of the reasons for establishing a firm oral basis in English before introducing the written medium, so that the child can learn what the language sounds like before he sees it written. Where circumstances demand some compromise, at least make sure that elementary-stage learners have met all words and syntax orally before they are required to read them.

In order to differentiate sounds from letters so that the reader knows which 'th' sound or which 'a' sound is meant, we use (i) key words to exemplify the sound in a word context and (ii) phonetic symbols. If you are not used to phonetic symbols you can ignore them and rely on the key words. The symbols are those used by Daniel Jones[1] and they are listed at the beginning and end of the book on the inside cover, together with key words.[2]

Regard this list as an inventory of English sounds, although in fact they represent the sounds of Southern English (sometimes called Received Pronunciation or RP). You may have a different accent – there is nothing particularly special about

---

[1] Daniel Jones, *The Pronunciation of English*, Heffer, 1964 (revised). You will find the same symbols used in Daniel Jones, *An English Pronouncing Dictionary*, J. M. Dent & Sons Ltd., 13th edition, 1967. This will be particularly useful for teachers who themselves are not native speakers.

[2] We have chosen to retain his original symbol ou in preference to ɔu which he uses in his 13th revised edition of *The Pronunciation of English*, and for typographical reasons, to use the symbol g instead of *g*.

Southern English – and this will mean that your vowel inventory will be slightly different to this one. On page 16 we have described some of the most notable differences within England but there is not room here to describe these in detail or to mention those found in Scotland, Wales or elsewhere. Nevertheless, the most important point will not be affected very much, and that is the matter of contrast. Even if you pronounce *bat* differently to the Southern English speaker, you will both make *bat* and *bet* sound different. Similarly, you will make word pairs like *live* and *leave* sound different. Much of the work in this book concerns contrasts, and these will be affected very little by differences of regional accent. RP has been chosen here in order to be consistent with other English language-teaching material.

Vowel sounds

Speakers vary in the number of different vowels they use, or to be more precise, in the number of different diphthongs. We consider that it is not necessary to introduce learners to all the optional ones and those shown here are sufficient for teaching purposes. You will find details of further possible diphthongs in Daniel Jones' book, *The Pronunciation of English*, page 98, if you are interested.

When vowel sounds are articulated, air is passed out of the lungs in a continuous flow, through the windpipe, the vocal cords vibrating and 'voicing' the vowel sound, and through the mouth. The position of the tongue, the lips, and to some extent the degree of jaw-opening gives to each vowel its distinctive quality. The relative length (or duration) of the vowel is also an important distinguishing point.

We can group the vowel sounds in different ways, relevant to teaching purposes:

1. PURE VOWELS AND DIPHTHONGS

Pure vowels:	i *bit*	i: *beat*
	e *bet*	ɑ: *barn*
	æ *bat*	ɔ: *bought*
	ʌ *but*	u: *boot*
	ɔ *pot*	ə: *bird*
	u *put*	
	ə *a(gain)*	

Diphthongs:	ei *bait*	iə *beer*
	ai *bite*	eə *bear*
	au *loud*	uə *tour* or *cure*
	ou *boat*	ɔə *door* or *oar*
	ɔi *boy*	

All vowels move slightly in practice; the mouth position changes and the quality of the vowel changes. This enables the speaker to progress smoothly from the preceding sound to the following one. But apart from this, pure vowels have a characteristic mouth position which is virtually held for the duration of the sound. Diphthongs however require a deliberate movement from one position to another, beyond any movement required to carry the speaker from the preceding sound to the following one. Like the pure vowel, however, the diphthong is contained in one syllable and it has no hiatus in the middle.

English has more diphthongs than most of the languages spoken by immigrants to Britain, and so this feature needs a great amount of practice. There are difficulties of three main kinds:

a. Some learners, particularly those from India and Pakistan, try to make diphthongs into pure vowels, remaining in the starting position of the diphthong and never moving away from it. This does not always prevent the speaker from being understood, but it is desirable to teach him to make true diphthongs. Failure to diphthongise ei and ou as in *bait* and *boat* respectively can cause confusion with other vowel sounds, although in some regions this pronunciation of *bait* and *boat* is normal.

b. Some learners, particularly Greek and Italian speakers, will be accustomed to pronouncing two separate vowel sounds in quick succession but making two syllables of them. You must help these children to get both sounds into the same syllable, by making the first vowel rather shorter and by reducing the energy of the second one.

c. Some learners, particularly Indians and Pakistanis, will tend to add r to diphthongs ending with the ə element (and also to long pure vowels). Although this does not happen in RP English, it does not affect intelligibility, and many other English accents have this feature in any case. It hardly matters therefore, and the time and energy that would be needed to eradicate it could be far better spent in other ways.

Some words – *hour* is an example – can be said either as one or as two syllables. When said as one, a triphthong is used, that is, a three-element vowel. Alternatively, we can use a diphthong and the neutral vowel, ə, making the word a two-syllabled one. For teaching this is usually an easier choice. Words like *mower*, *spire*, *player* and *lawyer* can also be said with triphthongs or given an extra syllable.

2. SHORT OR LONG VOWELS

Short vowels:		Long vowels:	
i	*bit*	iː	*beat*
ʌ	*but*	ɑː	*barn*
ɔ	*pot*	ɔː	*bought* or *port*
u	*put*	uː	*boot*
ə	*a(gain)*	əː	*bird*
e	*bet*	The diphthongs can also be thought
æ	*bat*	of as long.

The actual length of any vowel in continuous speech depends on the particular circumstances, for example, whether or not it is being stressed, what kind of sound follows, and if it is not being stressed how many other sounds also have to be fitted in between the two nearest stressed syllables. (See page 23 for notes on the rhythm and stressing of English.) The speed of delivery itself will obviously affect vowel length too. Nevertheless, other things being equal, some vowels are always relatively longer than others, and duration is an important distinguishing feature in pairs of words like *bit* and *beat*, *pot* and *port*.

When working on length contrasts, always choose examples where the vowel in question occurs in a stressed syllable, or if you are practising in sentences, see that the example word can be naturally stressed. In a position without stress, a vowel should always sound rather short and weak, and such examples would not show up length differences; even differences in quality are obscured.

Practise these length differences with all learners; the most difficult are those in *bit* and *beat* and in *pot* and *port*. Note that the two dots, (ː), indicate length, as in iː (*beat*).

3. VOWELS IN TERMS OF MOUTH POSITION

The features that are most important here are:

a. the lips, whether they are spread, rounded or neutral – that is, neither spread nor rounded. i: as in *beat* is a good example of a lip-spread vowel. Say it to yourself in a mirror and compare the lip position you need with that necessary for u: as in *boot*, a lip-rounded vowel. When teaching the following sounds it is often useful to exaggerate the lip position. These all have some tendency to lip-spreading:

i: *beat* i *bit*
ei *bait* e *bet*

u: as in *boot* is a good example of a lip-rounded vowel. Again, exaggeration is often a useful teaching device. These vowels have a tendency to lip-rounding:

ɔ: *bought* ɔi *boy* (to begin with)
ɔ *pot* ou *boat* (increasingly)
u *put* uə *tour* (slightly, at first)
u: *boot*

The other vowels require the lips to be in a relatively lax or neutral position.

b. The height of the tongue in the mouth. In both i: as in *beat* and u: as in *boot*, the tongue at its highest point is near the roof of the mouth. In æ as in *bat* and ɑ: as in *barn* the whole of the tongue is low in the mouth. The chart in the footnote shows these relative tongue positionings.[1]

c. These are the vowels where the tongue is higher at the front (front vowels):

i: as in *beat* e as in *bet*
i as in *bit* æ as in *bat*

These are the vowels where the tongue is higher at the back (back vowels):

u: as in *boot* u as in *put*
ɔ: as in *bought* ɔ as in *pot*
ɑ: as in *barn* (though not as far back as the vowels just mentioned.)

(Occasionally, variants of ʌ as in *but* though this should more properly be considered as a central vowel, along with ə: as in *bird* and ə as in *a(gain)*.)

---

[1] This chart shows the tongue position required for the vowels of English. Vowels like i: and u: require the tongue to be high in the mouth, but for i: the front of the tongue is the higher point (and it is therefore shown at the extreme left of this chart), while for u: the back of the tongue is the higher

Vowel sounds and rhythm

By far the most important vowel in English teaching and the one occurring most frequently in speech is ə as in *about*, first syllable, and in *mother*, second syllable. It is often called the neutral vowel because the tongue has to be in a neutral and lax position. In one study of vowel frequency, ə was found to account for 10% of all vowel occurrences, and the next most frequent vowel, e as in *bet*, accounted for only 2.97%.[1] This is confusing for the foreign learner for two reasons. One is that our spelling hardly suggests its existence, unless one counts the 'er' at the ends of words like *mother*. The other is that it occurs only in syllables that are not being stressed; so if the learner is not stressing his speech in the proper way, then either he will not be using this vowel at all, or he will be using it in the wrong places. Work on this vowel must therefore be related to questions of stressing right from the start. ə occurs in words of two kinds:

a. in words of more than one syllable, in a syllable that is never stressed, e.g. (*moth*)*er*, (*prob*)*a*(*bly*), *a*(*bout*).

---

point (and it is shown here at the extreme right of the chart). ə, being a 'neutral' vowel, and requiring the most central position of all, is shown right in the centre of the chart.

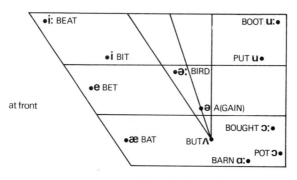

Chart showing position of the tongue

---

[1] B. B. Fry, in *Archives Néerlandaises de Phonétique Expérimentale*, XX (1947) pp. 103–6, and quoted by Gimson (p. 143).

b. in one-syllable words (usually structural words) which sometimes receive stress and sometimes do not, depending on the emphasis the speaker requires. When these words are stressed they are given one vowel sound (never ə), and when they are left unstressed they are given another vowel sound which is very often ə. i as in *bit* and u as in *put* are also used for these unstressed words, but less frequently than ə. Compare the way you would pronounce *the* in the two following cases:

1. *Here's* the *Prime Mi*nister.
2. *Do* you mean **the** *Har*old *Wil*son? (implying, 'or someone else with the same name?')

The does not usually get stressed – something to watch for in the first few weeks of English – and usually we say it lightly, quickly and unobtrusively, sometimes using i as in *bit* but more often ə, the neutral vowel. In sentence 2 above, however, *the* is given special significance and is therefore stressed. In order to do this we use a different vowel sound, i: as in *beat*.

If you stress the following sentence in the way indicated, leaving eight syllables unstressed, you can use ə for six of them quite naturally:

the *man* put the *bu*tter and *cheese* in the *cup*board

I have considered this vowel sound at some length, and at the risk of labouring it too much, because of its importance for natural English speech and because of the difficulties it raises for the learner. Its importance lies in its very unobtrusiveness, which serves to throw the stressed syllables of a sentence into greater relief; but the same unobtrusiveness often causes it to be overlooked in English teaching.

Stress, rhythm in general and intonation are considered specifically on page 23, but at this point I would also add, never imagine that you are helping a child by spea–king – slow–ly – and – e–ven–ly – with – e–v'ry – vo–wel – said – pre–ci–sely – and – e–qua–lly. Most of us have caught ourselves doing it at odd moments, but it is disastrously misleading to the learner. People just do not speak that way – under normal circumstances.

Regional variations within England

Vowels There are considerable differences between the normal speech of educated speakers in different parts of England, and especially in vowel sounds. A very rough division of the country into north and south by a line drawn south of Birmingham will serve as a basis for three very common vowel differences:

a. The vowel in *cat* is pronounced æ in the south, and in the north a. The northern vowel is made with the tongue slightly lower in the mouth, and is approximately the sound with which the diphthong ai as in *bite* begins. Learners in the north are therefore less likely to confuse words like *bat* and *bet*, but words like *bat* and *but* may be more confusing to them.

b. Many words, pronounced with a long ɑ: in the south, e.g. *bath, pass, last, dance*, are often pronounced in the north with a short a described in **a** above.

c. The vowel ʌ used in the south for words like *cut, bu(tter)*, *such*, etc., is not used by many northern speakers, who use the vowel they also use in *put, book, good* and *bu(tcher)* instead.

Also, though these differences are not necessarily geographically distributed, some speakers replace the diphthong ɛə as in *hair* with a long pure vowel ə: Many speakers in all regions do not distinguish between uə, ɔ: or ɔə (as in *tour, taught* and *drawer*), and pronounce all three with ɔ: as in *taught*. These are not, of course, the only differences, but they are particularly noticeable. Initially the learner may be confused when listening to you, if you are a southern speaker teaching in the north, or the other way around; but this confusion should not persist.

Consonants There is less regional variation in the pronunciation of consonants than in the case of vowels.

When consonant sounds are articulated, air is again passed out of the lungs through the windpipe. For one set of consonants the vocal cords are set in motion; these are the 'voiced consonants'. For the other consonants, the 'voiceless' ones, the vocal cords do not vibrate. (If you whisper a voiceless consonant, s or f for example, it sounds the same as when you speak it normally.) For some consonants the breath is allowed to flow continuously but its release is partially obstructed at some point and this produces an audible friction. Examples of these **fricatives** are f and v, s and z. The point at which this partial obstruction is made is crucial to the exact quality of the sound produced. In some consonants there is a total obstruction to the breath, which is then released with a slightly explosive effect. These are called **plosives**. p, b, t are examples.

Consonants can be grouped for teaching purposes according to the differences outlined above:

1. VOICED AND VOICELESS CONSONANTS

Voiceless consonants	Voiced consonants
p	b
t	d
k	g
θ (**th**in)	ð (**this**)
f	v
s	z
ʃ (**ship**)	ʒ (**measure**)
tʃ (**chin**)	dʒ (**gin**)
	m, n, ŋ (**sung**)
	w, r, l

For voiced consonants (and for all vowels) the vocal cords vibrate. Say zzzzzzzz or a prolonged ɑ: as in *cart*, place your fingers on your larynx and you will feel the vibration of the vocal cords.

Now change zzzzzzzz into sssssss, and as you change to the second sound you will find the vibration ceases. In teaching, it is useful to remember that many of the consonants come in pairs, voiced and voiceless, so that a student who can produce one of such a pair but not the other can be helped by being shown the relation between the two and by feeling his own larynx.

The larynx

2. THERE CAN BE DIFFERENT DEGREES OF FRICTION AND DIFFERENT WAYS OF AIR RELEASE.

i. p, b, t, d, k, g are **plosives**. They are formed by using the lips or tongue or velum as a barrier to prevent the breath escaping. This barrier is then released suddenly with a more or less explosive effect. (See 3 below for the different 'barriers' possible.)

ii. f, v, s, z, ʃ as in *ship*, ʒ as in *measure*, θ as in *thin*, ð as in *then*, and sometimes r are **fricatives**. These differ from the plosives in not having a complete barrier but instead a constriction through which the breath has to force a passage, resulting in an audible friction. These consonants can all be protracted, e.g. z——— or f———.

iii. tʃ as in *chip* and dʒ as in *gin* are called **affricates**. They make a complete barrier to the breath as do the plosives, but the breath is then released slowly so that a fricative effect follows on.

18

iv. w and j as in *you* are called **semi-vowels**. With these, as with vowels, the shape of the mouth cavity and the position of the tongue determine the characteristic sound quality of each. Lip position is important for w as well. They differ from vowels in the way in which they occur in the structure of syllables. It is therefore convenient to regard them as consonants, although if one describes them solely in phonetic terms, the difference is not clear cut.

v. l The air flow is continuous, but though it is impeded by the centre of the tongue, the obstruction is not great enough to produce audible friction. The air flows by on either one or both sides of the tongue. It is called a **lateral**.

vi. m, n and ŋ (*sing*). Air is prevented from escaping via the mouth, but the soft palate is lowered, enabling the air to escape through the nose. These are called **nasals**.

3. POINT WHERE BARRIER OR CONSTRICTION OCCURS

This is a diagram of the parts and organs of the mouth and throat crucial to the production of the different sounds in our speech:

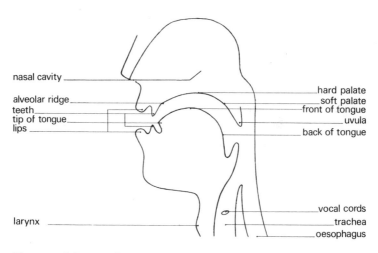

Diagram of the mouth

i. In p and b and m, the *lips* form the barrier. These are called **bilabials**.

ii. In f and v, the *upper teeth and lower lip* make the constriction. These are called **labiodentals**.

iii. In θ and ð as in *thin* and **then**, the *upper teeth and tongue* are responsible. These are called **dentals**.

iv. In t, d, s, z, n, l, the *alveolar ridge and tongue* are responsible. These are called **alveolars**.

v. In r, the *tongue* and a point slightly further back *beyond the alveolar ridge* are responsible. This is called a **post-alveolar**.

vi. In tʃ and dʒ as in *chin* and *gin* and ʃ and ʒ as in *ship* and *measure*, the *tongue* and a *point slightly further back* still are responsible. These are called **palato-alveolars**.

vii. In k, g and ŋ as in *sing* the *tongue* and *soft palate* are responsible. These are called **velars**.

viii. In h, the *glottis* is partly responsible, but there is also a general friction further forward, and the exact position is influenced by the vowel that follows. This is called a **glottal**.

NB. The semi-vowels j as in *you* and w have more in common with vowels, in this respect. j is formed in a position similar to i, and w resembles u.

It is useful to understand the similarities and differences between the various consonant sounds, because a learner may be having great difficulty with a sound which is in fact closely related to another which he can manage easily; this means you can show him how to progress from a manageable sound to a problem one. Do not theorise about mouth position and consonant type where you can avoid it, although there are always occasions when it is helpful. The only parts of the speech organs that can be seen in action are the lips (their shape and how, if at all, they are affecting breath release) and the teeth. It may therefore be useful to draw attention to these. A hand mirror is sometimes useful. One can also draw attention to voicing or nonvoicing because the larynx can be felt vibrating for voiced sounds, especially when the sound is one that can be prolonged, like s, z or any of the vowels.

2 Putting sounds together

Pronunciation involves much more than simply mastering component sounds, and many difficulties begin only when the speaker tries to put them together in words, phrases and connected speech. This book tries to show how pronunciation work must start and end with connected continuous speech, but that sometimes it is necessary to practise individual words or even individual sounds as one step in the process.

Connected speech confronts the learner with two main kinds of pronunciation difficulty. One is that certain sequences of sounds will feel unnatural to him and will require practice. The other is that of mastering the speech rhythms of English. The rhythm is of great importance.

Specific sound combinations

Consonant clusters There are no English words beginning with the consonant cluster ks although you often find this cluster at the end of a word, as in *makes*. There are no words with str at the end, although you often find it at the beginning, as in *street*. Speakers of some Indian languages, for example, Punjabi, are not used at all to clusters like str. We are all used to certain sounds occurring together but not others, and we are used to them occurring in only certain positions. So in a new language clusters will tend to cause difficulty at first, even when the component consonants are individually manageable. Difficulties may be of several types:

1. The learner may react to the difficulty by 'changing' the position of the cluster in the word, so that it is easier for him; he may do this by adding an initial vowel to an initial cluster, so that a word like *stop* becomes 'istop', a cluster preceded by a vowel being manageable for him; or with a final cluster, he may add an extra vowel, making *help* into 'helpa'.

2. He may split up the cluster into a series: consonant, vowel, consonant, vowel, etc., making as many extra syllables as there are extra vowels, words like *street* becoming 'satareet'. *Stop* may also become 'sitop'. This is the Punjabi child's solution.

3. He may rearrange the consonants to make the cluster more manageable; *desk* sometimes becomes 'deks' for example.

4. He may change some of the consonants completely; Greek learners tend to say words like *blackboard*, where the central cluster consists of a voiceless and a voiced consonant, as 'blagboard', making both consonants voiced.

Rapid speech produces similar clusters between words, as in *watch this*. These can be equally difficult and need practice. We do not say 'Watch – (pause) – this', unless we are being very emphatic; the two words follow smoothly. Native speakers make things easier for themselves by adjusting some of these sounds slightly for every particular sound context. Just as unstressed vowel sounds get legitimately 'skimped' in order to accommodate them in the rhythm pattern (see page 23), some consonant sounds in clusters such as *What's she saying* also get skimped or eliminated, to make it possible for the speaker to fit everything in smoothly and rhythmically. This is normal and acceptable among native speakers; and although, carried to excess, it would give a slovenly effect, such reduction is normal and sometimes necessary in rapid conversational speech, where too many successive consonants pile up in interword clusters. Of course, when we are speaking particularly emphatically, we take trouble to say things much more clearly, and, necessarily, more slowly. But nobody speaks like that all the time; even the orator is selective in his emphasis. This should not be made an important teaching point in itself, but there will be the occasion, perhaps in dialogue work or in a rhyme, or in a difficult sequence of sounds arising in any situation, when it is useful to teach the shortened version deliberately. In speech, many things are sacrificed to rhythmic momentum. This is another reason why it is important to speak to the children at your natural pace; if you always speak unnaturally carefully and rather slowly to them, they are going to find it hard to understand everyone else.

Incomplete plosion This feature is found in certain clusters and must be taught, although not as a first priority. Examples can be found in words like *blackboard*, *postman* and *clock*. Here, the k in *blackboard*, the t in *postman*, and the first k in *clock* are not pronounced fully. Although the mouth takes up the right position, the air-release is postponed and made with the consonant following. Failure to do this will leave the learner trying to articulate two consonant sounds that are very hard to say smoothly in succession. In words like *blackboard*, the central cluster involves two plosive consonants, k and b (see page 18 for plosives). In such cases we adjust our mouth to a position for b before we have completed k. Instead of releasing a little breath for k, and then doing the same for b, the breath for k is held on and released with b. Other examples of this appear in *first class*, *bedtime*, etc. Alternatively, the t (in *first class*) and the d (in *bedtime*) may disappear entirely. In words like *postman* with a plosive and a nasal, a similar thing happens, but the breath for t is released nasally with m, as also in *quick note*, *pocke-t money*, and *ribbon* (where the final vowel virtually

disappears in many cases). In words like *clock*, the breath for k
is released laterally over the side of the tongue with l, and also
in *lamplight*, *plastic*, and *bottle*. (*bottle* can be pronounced as
virtually one syllable – or let us say, one and a half).

Rhythm and Intonation

Rhythm This is one of the most important features of connected
speech, yet it is often neglected in the classroom. Many
languages give equal weight and timing to each syllable. The
effect resembles the tapping of a fast, even typist, or of a
machine gun, rat-tat-tat-tat, etc. Some languages give differen-
tial stress to syllables within the words, but do not also have an
overall pattern of sentence stressing. English has a two-tier
stress system, and the speaker who does not observe this, even
though his speech is correct in many respects, will be very hard
to follow, because no landmarks rise above the torrent of sound,
and the vowel sounds become especially distorted. Fortunately
it is one of the easier features to improve.

Word stress Usually words of more than one syllable are said
with stress on the same syllable. We always say *al*ways, never
al*ways*. We always say al*though*, never *al*though. The difficulty
here is remembering how to stress individual words; there are
few simple rulings that can be given to the student to help him,
so make sure that when a child is learning a new word he learns
its stress pattern too.

Sentence stress In connected speech, word stress is overlaid by
sentence stress. This is a matter of what stands out in any
particular sentence, and it depends on the intention of the
speaker. Any sentence can be stressed in many ways; the only
proviso is that the word stress must not get distorted in the
process. The internal stressing of a word not given sentence
stress on that occasion may be barely audible, as in '*we'll*
probably *come*' (where you can hardly make out the internal
stress of probably).

The number of stressed syllables that occur in a particular
sentence is connected with – among other things – speed of
speech. A sentence like 'Did you see him?' might also be
stressed in a number of ways, each one making a different
implication. Consider:

1. *Did* you *see* him? (Or did you only speak to him on the
phone?)

2. Did *you* see him? (Or was it only Joe that saw him?)
3. *Did* you see *him*? (Or did you only see her?)
4. *Did you see him*? (Answer me. I am getting angry.)

The speaker who does not stress his speech clearly is very difficult to follow. He may seem to be gabbling if he speaks at a normal rate or faster, and if he speaks slowly he will be most monotonous and difficult to listen to.

Stressed syllables in a sentence come at roughly equal intervals of time, regardless of the number of unstressed syllables between them. You may find two consecutive stresses as in 4 above, or two stresses with one intervening syllable as in 1 above, or with two intervening syllables as in 3 above. It is rare to find more than two intervening syllables in slow deliberate speech as in much elementary language work, though we do make some stresses heavier than others, according to their significance in the whole communication. In more rapid speech, however, we often pack in three, four or more unstressed syllables between stresses.

In order to bring out the difference between stressed and unstressed syllables and to squeeze in the unstressed syllables without distorting the rhythm, a learner must be able to make clear contrasts between long and short vowels. He will need rhythm practice and vowel practice and he will need help with tricky consonant clusters. Many learners do not make use of ə the neutral vowel. Thus the failure to make important words and syllables stand out and the failure to use very short neutral vowels where they are needed in unstressed positions are connected and need to be tackled together. The monosyllabic words that change their vowel sound in unstressed position are mainly structural words, pronouns like *he*, *she* and *you*, conjunctions like *and* and *but*, auxiliary verb forms like *been*, *have* and *were*, prepositions like *for* and *to*. Say the two following sentences with the stress suggested and as naturally as possible, and compare the way you pronounce *to* in each case:

1. He was **go**ing to **Brad**ford
2. He was **go**ing **to Brad**ford. (Implication: not coming away from it.)

The exact pronunciation of unstressed vowels is not important: in fact it varies; but it is very important that the speaker should be able to make the most significant words and syllables stand out, by giving their vowels full weight and skating lightly over remaining vowels and syllables.

Intonation By intonation we mean the speech 'tune'. As in music this depends for its shape on the underlying rhythm. If the rhythm is wrong the intonation will sound strange. Intonation helps to draw attention to important points and also to add information to the utterance, particularly about the speaker's attitudes; it can soften an otherwise rather stark utterance, making it gentler or more polite; or it can make it more authoritative, or urgent, express humour, doubt; and so on.

There are several ways of representing intonation on paper. We have tried to avoid specifying intonation in this book and in *Scope, Stage One* because, since there is wide variation from individual to individual and situation to situation, it is more satisfactory for the teacher to look to his or her own speech for a model for the class to imitate. It is also very difficult to speak with an intonation pattern prescribed for you by someone else, and even harder to 'read' it. The method we have used in one or two places is shown below. Dashes represent stressed syllables, dots represent unstressed syllables. The pitch of the voice is shown by the position of the dashes between the upper and lower stave lines.

Here are examples of the Up Tune and the Down Tune.

Up Tune

Is it mine?

Down Tune

John's gone to find him

Thus, in *Is it mine?* the tune starts high on *is*, and falls to its lowest point on the beginning of *mine*, shooting up again on that syllable. This is an example of the Up Tune. In *John's gone to find him*, we have an example of the Down Tune. It starts high on the first stressed syllable, which happens to also be the first syllable of the sentence, *John's*. The second stressed syllable here is *gone*, and the tune has fallen a little in pitch. The third stress is *find*, and on this syllable the tune falls as far as it is going to. The final syllable, *him*, is unstressed, and stays in pitch somewhere near the finishing point of *find*. Note that the stressed syllables are the ones that really carry the tune; the unstressed syllables just 'hang on'.

B

Sometimes intonation has a grammatical function; compare the two following sentences:

His name is Rufus.
His name is Rufus?

On paper, the punctuation alone tells us that the second one is a question. In speech, intonation would show the difference.

One difficulty in teaching intonation lies in the fact that it varies greatly between individual speakers and in different speech situations; generalisations can be very misleading. Nevertheless, it is important to attune the learner's ear to certain contrasts basic to English intonation, and the best way of doing this is to make him imitate your own intonation when doing oral exercises and drills and especially when practising dialogues. Your examples must necessarily be consistent, if he is to imitate you, so a tape recording will be helpful. You will find that colourful intonations catch on quickest, so do not hesitate to exaggerate and to over-dramatise. Most of the children will water your example down when reproducing it. A child who feels slightly foolish when trying to reproduce a certain intonation will usually feel more at ease when he appreciates its significance for a particular situation.

One broad contrast that the learner should be taught to recognise in the speech of others, in order to detect questions and whether or not a speaker has finished, is the contrast between utterances finishing on a falling tune and those that finish on a rising one. Most learners will have to be trained to hear this difference, and it is important. 'Down Tune' utterances tend to imply definiteness, authority, and a sense of 'plain speaking'. 'Up Tune' utterances often indicate that something more is needed, perhaps a short confirmation or denial by the listener, or that the speaker is going to continue, or that he wishes to imply something that he cannot say, perhaps doubt. The 'Up Tune' can also make an otherwise bare utterance sound more polite, reassuring, or gentle. Used where these feelings are not appropriate, it can sound weak or apologetic. The Up Tune is very often used for questions.

3 Techniques –
How to teach pronunciation

In Pronunciation Work, as in any kind of teaching, a lot of individual attention is necessary, and circumstances prevent us from giving as much of this as we would like; but although much can be done with groups, and some work even with the whole class, you will often have to draw one or two children aside for special help. However you organise your work, see that each child has frequent and regular opportunities to work on his particular pronunciation difficulties, when he can devote all his attention to them rather than to the other matters of vocabulary, grammar, etc.

One has constantly to be tuned to pronunciation difficulties, to spot problems and watch progress. When the class is learning a new language pattern, or practising a pattern repetitively in a drill, pay as much attention to their rhythm and intonation as to the grammatical detail. Teach them to listen for this right from the beginning and to keep it in mind. Try to get the children to imitate you for the complete effect of what you say, sounds, rhythm, intonation and all; but also give them help in these things separately, in the ways suggested in the following sections. If you have been working on individual sounds or individual words, always follow up with some sentence practice, preferably relating the point at issue to other language work that you are doing currently. The sentences need not be tongue-twisters. One or two occurrences of the problem features in each sentence are quite enough. An example relevant to the class's current interests is far better than one thought up by someone else.

1 Planning pronunciation work

Your work should fall into the following categories:

a. Maintaining the class's attention to pronunciation in an overall sense: encouraging them to imitate your rhythm and intonation patterns in oral exercises, drills, and dialogues; slowing them down if they begin to gabble; noting problems with individual sounds or sound combinations.

b. Practising important items like names and addresses, and in due course, basic information about each child, since he will be asked for it frequently.

c. Exercises designed to develop the rhythmic and melodic sense.

d. Sentence and dialogue practice. Use these to find out the problem spots, to practise the difficult sounds and sound combinations in continuous speech and also to check on progress made.

e. Practising individual sounds and sound combinations that are difficult (preferably in words, not in isolation). Always follow this up with practice in sentences and link it to other current language work.

Note that all these five categories need *continual* attention, and such work must be brisk and lively. Never let it drag.

2   **Attitudes to speechwork**

Establish the idea among the children that pronunciation is important, and that everyone has problems and no one need feel hypersensitive on that account. Over-anxiety on the children's part may cause its own problems, especially as the Indian languages require greater tension of the mouth muscles than English. It is impossible to make English sound natural if your muscles are tied up in knots.

Sometimes it is worth while to break off what you are doing, and to relax the class completely. An occasional breathing exercise is very useful here, disguised as a game, or not, as you prefer. One breathing 'game' which gets young children drawing in deep breaths and releasing them slowly and steadily is the Fish Race. Cut fish shapes out of flimsy paper, so that each child has a fish. Then let the fishes be raced across the floor by steadily blowing – no hands allowed. The secret is to blow evenly, and not to huff and puff haphazardly. If you do not have enough floor space for this, cut out birds, butterflies or leaves instead, and get the children to hold them just in front of their mouths, so that they flutter when they breathe out.

28

3   Diagnosing problems

Many of the children's pronunciation problems will be
immediately noticeable. Note them down, either by using a
phonetic notation, or alternatively by writing down a word or
word group in which the problem arises, circling the offending
part and perhaps adding a qualifying note. Many problems
concern pairs of sounds, and for these, write down an example
of the pair to illustrate the difficulty, e.g. *thin/tin*.
In addition to highly noticeable difficulties, there will also
be a number of smaller faults, significant because their cumula-
tive effect is to reduce intelligibility. (See the notes on the basic
sound system of English on page 9.) Your first priority should
be to ensure that the child is not confusing any of the sounds
of English or producing them so that they are unrecognisable to
the non-specialist ear. (It is possible for him to have a strong
'foreign accent' without being difficult to understand.) The
notes in Part Two will help you establish these priorities.
A tape recorder will make it easier for you to listen carefully
to each child's speech. If you build up an archive of recordings
it will enable you to compare different samples of a child's
speech over a period of time, and to assess his progress more
accurately, and you will find it extremely useful to be able to
refer back to old cases in the future. When making these
tapes, note the name of the child, his native language, his
length of time in Britain and in your class, and the date.
Reading aloud is a distinct and a very exacting skill in itself,
and not necessarily a good indication of the child's intelligibility
in speech; dialogues which the children understand, enjoy and
have learned by heart would be suitable for this purpose.

4   How often to correct pronunciation

This must inevitably be a matter of your own discretion and
close knowledge of each child. However, a few general points
can be made. Do not harass a child by continually stopping and
correcting him. This applies even to specific speechwork
sessions. In these sessions focus your attention on the points
you have decided to work on. There will often be other mistakes
that you will want to comment on or correct then and there,
but do not do this more than necessary; make a note of points
that do not satisfy you and then have a go at them later. The
same applies to other language work. Do not interrupt the child

whenever he opens his mouth and produces a sound that falls short of your expectations. Otherwise correct the child only if he is obviously not trying or is reverting to an old fault. But do listen to what he does, and listen especially to how he manages points that you have been working on in pronunciation sessions, because the real test of his improvement comes when he is using language for a 'real purpose'.

Be quick to show approving recognition of even faint improvement and effort, but progress will mostly be a long-term process; sudden dramatic improvement is unusual.

5   The mechanics of pronunciation work

CHILD: *sell*
TEACHER: *shell*
CHILD: *sell*
TEACHER (patiently): *shell*
CHILD: *sell*
TEACHER (more patiently): *shell*
CHILD: *sell*
TEACHER (less patiently): *shell*
CHILD: *sell*

This child needs to practise recognising the differences between the two words *shell* and *sell* and other pairs contrasting these two consonant sounds. He will not be able to produce them distinctly himself until he can *hear* the difference between them, when you say them.

Whatever kind of point you are working on, there are four processes through which each child must have a chance to work: **listening, imitating, experimenting** and **practising**.

a.   Listening This is the essence of the ear training work outlined in Part Two. It is not enough to assume that a child has 'heard' the sound (or intonation pattern, or whatever it may be) simply because it has been going on around him. He must be brought face to face with it, and then with potentially confusing contrasts. Recognising contrasts is very important. Get him to tell you whether word pairs like *shell/sell* are the same or different. Ask him to spot words with 'sh' in them. If you find a child cannot produce two distinct sounds, you will probably find he cannot hear the difference in the first place. He must be fully aware of what he is trying to produce, and this is impossible until he has listened to it with his undivided attention. See page 36 for details of how to practise this.

b. Imitating and experimenting These two processes are distinct but go together, and are a necessary first step in production work. The child must be able to imitate you and to experiment, in an unconstrained atmosphere, without feeling self-conscious. Consider the amount of experimenting a baby learning his first language has to do; and the baby is in a far better position to learn a language than the second-language learner. Do not allow a child to go on and on at something where he is making no progress; try another approach, or leave it and return to it later. It is useful if older children can become (constructively) critical of each other; but of course this must not become competitive, or it will do the weaker ones more harm than good.

The information in Part One on individual sounds is for your benefit, and it is not intended that it should be passed on to the child. It is better not to theorise very much about pronunciation, even when the child can understand explanations, but to rely on auditory *and* visual imitation. Even when explanations can be understood and the interest exists, there is still a leap to be made, to put theory to practice and to produce the desired result. People are simply not accustomed to arranging their mouths in unfamiliar positions unless they have been specially trained to do so.

The experimenting stage involves experiment, trial and error, on your part as well as on the children's. Sometimes you will find that an apparently ludicrous and unscientific suggestion gets just the right reaction from the learner. Try exaggeration, gestures, drawing attention to teeth, lip or tongue position, or to voicing, to length or shortness, or to the changing quality of a diphthong. You may need to make a funny face, or to pretend to 'be' something that 'makes' the sound you require, e.g. 'ssssssss' (a snake), or 'th th th' θ (someone pumping up a tyre). Small hand mirrors can be very useful in enabling children to see the position of their lips. Let the general atmosphere be as relaxed and uninhibited as possible. Once the child has stumbled on the correct sound or pattern, you have both made a major break-through, because at last he knows what it *feels* like. Get him to do it two or three times more, and then stop and try again later in the day, and the next day, until he can produce it to order.

c. Practice This process will continue indefinitely. It would be unrealistic to hope for perfection; the important thing is that the child should be aware of his particular trouble spots, and should be trying. The ultimate test is how he speaks in moments of excitement and when other things are competing for his attention.

6 How to work on rhythm and intonation

Rhythm work

The rhythm and intonation of English have been described on pages 23–26. It is most important for all learners to work at these features, especially in the early stages. Incorrect rhythm is one of the greatest causes of unintelligibility.

The following activities will help develop rhythmic sense:

1. Musical activity Bring in as much of this as possible, using for this purpose western music with a strong rhythmic character. It is a good idea to get help from another teacher if music is not your strong point. Any or all of the following musical activities will be helpful in developing a rhythmic sense:

1. Listening
2. Movement to music: P.E. and dancing of all kinds
3. Singing[1]
4. Playing musical instruments, however crudely. Improvised percussion bands will be popular with the children if not with the teacher next door.

2. Rhymes and verse Select material that is not too difficult to understand and which does not involve old-fashioned, or highly idiosyncratic or stylised language. Also try to ensure that the rhythm of the rhyme reflects correct speech rhythm and does not 'fight' it as, for example, in bad limericks. You will find some rhymes and songs at the end of the book, page 151.

3. Rhythm beating Suggestions are given in page 148–9 and in *Scope, Stage One*. This accustoms the children to the regular spacing of strong beats and to interspersing different numbers

---

[1] See J. Dakin, *Songs and Rhythm for the Teaching of English*, Pupils' Book, and Teacher's Book, Longman, 1968.

of weak beats. It also develops rhythmic memory. Beating simple musical rhythms can lead to beating sentence rhythms. Most teachers find that this kind of work takes a little time to get established, but pays dividends in the long run and provides great enjoyment. The musical rhythms should be beaten for the children first; they should then join in, and finally beat on their own. A very quick class might divide into two groups, each beating a different rhythm. The sentence rhythms should also be demonstrated first, but aim for the children to be able to beat the rhythm of any sentence that you have repeated twice. Also practise beating the rhythm of sentence patterns and phrases that you teach.

Speech is not in fact quite as rhythmically regular as music and rhyme, but it is sufficiently so for this kind of rhythmic work to be extremely valuable. If you can get the children to place their stressed syllables at approximately even time-intervals, it will be a valuable achievement. See page 23. You will find that you have to exaggerate rhythm, but this will serve as a necessary corrective to the children's tendency to give the same stress to each syllable, to their lack of rhythmic momentum and to their mistakes in stressing individual words. An additional feature that you could show a good receptive class is the slight slowing up at the end of a final or isolated sentence. This reduces the feeling of abruptness. Be careful to use language material with which the children are familiar, and no new words or structures.

Rhythms are represented in *Scope Stage One* and in the following pages by means of *dah* for strong beats and *di* for weak ones. Do not let the children *say* the rhythms as *dah dah di dah*, etc. or read sentences for early rhythm work or they will use a flat or an unnatural intonation which will be bad practice. Let them listen and then simply beat the rhythms. Two fingers beating on the palm of the hand is an effective but not too noisy means of doing this. Finally, let them say the sentences, using the right rhythm, and imitating your intonation as far as possible. Some teachers have found it useful to draw a series of squares on the blackboard, to show the rhythm of each set of sentences. Thus, □ ▫ ▫ □ □ ▫ □ would represent the rhythm of *Where* is the *new box* of *chalk*? The more you can get the children to rely on their ears, however, the better.

Whenever you are doing repetitive oral exercises or drills, try to bring out the language rhythm; this will increase the value and the interest of the exercise.

Intonation

This is closely related to rhythm. If the rhythm is wrong, a speaker's intonation will sound strange. Languages vary in the variety of intonation patterns they permit and in the significance they attach to them; English is very rich in this respect. Intonation patterns are not cross-cultural, so it is not always safe to assume that you can convey your meaning to a new arrival by your tone of voice; he may interpret it differently. The best way to improve a child's intonation is to encourage him to imitate native models; and you, as his teacher, are the most convenient one. Do make use of recordings of other speakers, though, to introduce variety and to widen the children's experience. Incidentally, do not worry if, in comparing notes with fellow teachers, you find you cannot agree on what intonation to give a particular sentence. There is a wide range of possible variation and we express our personalities by the kind of intonation we use. You will soon find the children are expressing their own personalities through their intonation, despite the fact that they have used your intonation as a model originally.

The following activities will be helpful:

1. Singing and playing instruments Choose easy and attractive tunes, with plenty of repetition. Avoid awkward intervals, tricky rhythms and difficult key changes. This will help develop a sense of relative pitch and the melodic memory.[1]

2. Repetitive language work Whether you use drills or language games for this, they will be the more useful and enjoyable if you encourage colourful and expressive intonation. Exaggerate yourself, in order to project the intonation across to the children and to attract their attention. You will find that colourful and dramatic examples catch on quickest.

3. Dialogues These are indispensable in practising intonation, because they show intonation at work in miniature situations, where relationships are sketched out. Immigrant children can sound rude because of their intonation, and reasonable

---

[1] See J. Dakin, *Songs and Rhymes for the Teaching of English*, Longman, 1968. This is useful for all learners, and the Teacher's Book is especially helpful. W. R. Lee and M. Dodderidge, *Time for a Song*, Longman, 1963, is most suitable for younger children who are not beginners in English.

intonation can certainly make all the difference between a fair and a good speaker of English. Teach a short dialogue from a tape, encouraging the children to imitate the intonation. A large group at different stages in English can be involved in the same dialogue, if you give the harder parts to the more advanced, the easier parts to the newer children. The more advanced can also help by demonstrating a dialogue to newer pupils, and can help in teaching it. Everyone will want a turn, however, or some will become bored, and there will have to be a rapid turnover of performers. It is often useful to contrast a particular example of intonation that you want the children to use in a dialogue with an obviously inappropriate example, to show the relevance of this aspect of expression: if possible, make it amusing.

Any dramatic work, including dance and mime without any speech, is valuable in building up a child's confidence, giving him ability to express himself spontaneously and to project his personality, and above all, to experiment under the protection of a 'pretend' situation. An uninterested, shy or reluctant child should never be forced into this kind of activity, but rather allowed to watch and then join in when he feels inclined to do so – which will probably be when he thinks everyone else is preoccupied. Similarly, older children should not be made to feel insulted or foolish by work they feel is beneath their dignity, or irrelevant to the serious business of education. Yet this is a matter of personalities rather than age, and older classes can enjoy and benefit from this kind of work. The secret is to discover a theme which intrigues them particularly.

Here are some suggestions: a sports theme, perhaps following a spectacular television broadcast, some kind of dance movement, activity at a fair, at a circus or in a market, kinds of farm work, different operations seen on a building site, different kinds of people in the High Street shopping on Saturday morning; or a piece of music, film, a story, poem, picture, or some actual incident. Try also to tap the children's former experience in their country of origin and their own store of traditions and folk tales.[1]

---

[1] See Alan G. James, *Stories from the Punjab*, article in *English for Immigrants*, the Journal of the Associations of Teachers for the Education of Pupils from Overseas (A.T.E.P.O.), OUP, Vol. 2. 1970.

7 How to work on individual sounds and sound combinations

To summarise, difficulties in producing particular sounds often result from inability to recognise them in the speech of others. Listening and aural discrimination work are most important. Do not isolate a problem sound unless you have to, but work with words that contain it. Use words that are familiar, and never ask the children to read them; let them use their ears. Reading in any case involves further pronunciation hazards, because the spelling will mislead, and also because they will find it hard when reading aloud to stress correctly and to use weak forms of words like *the*, *a*, *he*, etc. This is another reason why you should delay introducing reading until they are familiar with the sound of the language and have a firm basis of oral language.

Ear training

The ear training material you will find in Part Two is of two kinds:

a. The child has to discriminate between two sounds; he is given pairs of words, some of which are the same, some different. An exercise to practise distinguishing between the two vowel sounds i: and i as in *sheep* and *ship* might go as follows:

TEACHER:	*sheep, ship*. Are they the same or different?
	sheep, ship.
CHILD:	Different (*or*, they're different.)
TEACHER:	Yes, that's right.
	sheep, sheep. sheep, sheep.
CHILD:	The same.
TEACHER:	Yes, good.
	ship, ship. ship, ship.
CHILD:	The same.

etc.

Eventually, you will want the children to be able to get the right answer after only one hearing.

Although the practice material in Part Two invariably offers several word pairs like this – usually called 'minimal pairs' – one pair is quite sufficient material for one session. When the children can discriminate accurately, get them to practise producing the words themselves.

b. The children have to spot the given sound whenever it occurs

36

in a series of words that you say to them. This kind of exercise is not quite as useful as the minimal pair exercise described above, but is nevertheless worthwhile when the children do not have a large enough vocabulary for you to find minimal pairs, or where such pairs do not exist. An exercise of this kind, to practise distinguishing f and v, might go as follows:

TEACHER: I'm going to say a list of words, Listen for words with f.[1] *Four, four.* Is there f in *four*?
CHILD: Yes.
TEACHER: Right. *Van, van.* Is there f in *van*?
CHILD: No.
TEACHER: Right. *Foot, foot.*
CHILD: Yes.
TEACHER: *Half, half.*
CHILD: Yes.
TEACHER: Yes, there was f at the end.

In due course you will want the children to be able to get the right answer after only one hearing of each word. In the example above, the sound f does not only occur at the beginning of words; one of the words ends with it.

As suggested in *Scope, Stage One* teach the expressions *the same* and *different* fairly early. They are essential to pronunciation work and will be useful for all kinds of other classroom activities.

Both types of exercise can be made into a game, and both can be used with small groups or larger ones. The children can respond in turn round the class, or all simultaneously, putting up hands when they think a pair of words are identical and laying them on the desk if they think they are different; or, in the second type of exercise, they can shoot up their hands whenever they hear the given sound. The second type can be played round the class on the principle of the old counting game, *Buzz*. A word is said to each child in turn. If he hears the sound in it, he must say 'Buzz' or 'Yes'. Traditionally you are 'out' if you make a mistake; but to avoid eliminating all the weaker children first and thus giving them less practice when they need more, you might reverse the process, making them stay 'in' if wrong, letting them 'out' of the game when they have a score of three correct responses. Keep a tally on the board. Older children can be got to write numbers on to a piece

---

[1] Say 'fff', not 'ef', because you are talking about sounds and not letters.

of paper and to put a tick against the appropriate number when they hear identical pairs or the given sound in a word. For more advanced children and with certain sound pairs, you can invent amusing sentences, and ask them to tell you which are nonsense and which are possible, e.g. when practising the difference between i: and i as in *sheep/ship*.

the sheep was on the sea (Wrong)
the sheep was in the field (Right)
etc.

Ear training lends itself to work with tape recorders, whether or not you have sets of individual headphones. If you number the 'cues' and give the children numbered papers, you can ask them to place ticks when they hear a particular sound (or a pair of identical words), and then you can check their performance afterwards. Otherwise you have no means of knowing whether or not they were simply reinforcing mistakes.

Production

Whatever their age, the children will need a chance to experiment with sounds. This is best done in groups of about three, so that you can hear what each child is saying and thus steer him in the right direction without making him feel you are breathing down his neck, ready to pounce as soon as he opens his mouth. Production work really has to be done in small groups, if weaker children are to receive the help and encouragement they need.

It is important not to introduce the written word in pronunciation work. Phonic work in reading is important, but there your focus is rather different, so do not try to make phonic reading work serve the two purposes; keep reading out of pronunciation work. Where you feel you will make enough use of them, prepare sets of pictorial cue cards, e.g. for æ and e pictures of a cat, bat, bed, hen, pen, hat, etc. See also the Picture Book for *Scope, Stage One*, page 24, which has pictures for pronunciation practice of this work. Some of the *Scope, Stage One* Picture Cards will also be useful for such work with small groups of children.

You will have to rely mostly on giving the children words to say after you or from tape. This is a perfectly feasible exercise, however, as a child who invariably mispronounces a sound will probably do it even when imitating you, because he cannot recognise the difference, and may not yet have found the way to produce it. Where you have a small group of older children working on the same problem, encourage them to listen critically to each other; this must be done in a helpful spirit rather than in cut-throat competition.

As suggested earlier, where you need to isolate problem sounds with younger children, try to make it into a game. Think of something that 'makes' that sound. Thus, a snake will say 'ssssssss', an insect 'zzzzzzzz'. For 'Shhhhh' you can pretend to quieten the baby or get quiet for Father who is sleeping, for 'th th th th' (as in *thin*) you can pump up a tyre. The exit of the steam train is a great loss, for we can no longer say 'tsh tsh tsh' is a train, since some children may never have heard steam engines. Pneumatic doors on new buses often make this noise, though as a continuous sound. Animal noises are useful for vowel sounds too, although animals conventionally 'say' different things from language to language. Nevertheless, you can discuss such differences and pursue your pronunciation work through the English examples. It is essential to follow up sound practice in words with sound practice in sentences, because here a child has to combine correct sound production with correct rhythm, and the two go closely together. Remember that vowel contrasts are crucial in stressed syllables, but matter very little in unstressed ones. Consonant contrasts matter everywhere, but should be said particularly clearly and prominently at the beginning of stressed syllables. But above all, make sure that important syllables stand out, and that unimportant syllables do *not*.

Combinations of sounds that in themselves are not difficult often require special attention. This may involve a familiar consonant in an unfamiliar place in the word or it may involve a sequence of difficult consonant sounds (see page 21).

Problems with clusters are various: here are some suggestions for working on them:

a. A sound may be in an unfamiliar position in the word. Thus d at the end of a word can be a problem to an Italian because although he can manage d, no Italian words end with d, and few end with consonants at all. In such a case, first make sure that the d sound is not a problem in itself. Practise a few words with d elsewhere. If simple imitation does not produce an acceptable pronunciation of a word like *lid*, ending with d, allow the child to say it with the additional final vowel sound that he feels he needs to say; then get him to split the word into two, *lid-* vowel. Then get him to drop the vowel altogether. This 'splitting' technique can also be used for difficult clusters of consonants.

b. If the child is 'changing' one or more of the component consonants to make it manageable for himself, practise by building up the cluster gradually until he can negotiate the whole thing in the context of a sentence and get the rhythm right as well.

c. If he is reversing the order of component consonants, for example, saying 'deks' for *desk*, practise in the same way: 'des', k; 'Des-k'; and then 'desk'.

d. The child may be splitting up the cluster, by inserting vowel sounds between the component consonants, e.g. he may be saying 'miluk' for *milk*, and in the process creating an extra syllable. First dispose of the extra vowel. Practice 'mil' and practise k. Practise 'mil-k' seeing that the vowel does not reappear, and gradually unite into *milk*. When you move on to practising words like this in sentences, make the children beat out the rhythm as well.

---

8 Saying names and addresses clearly

It is worth while to devote some attention to helping the children to say their names and addresses slowly and clearly. You obviously cannot Anglicise their pronunciation of their own names, but do encourage them to say them very slowly. Explain to the children that it is as hard for us to hear and say *their* names as it is for them to hear and say *ours*, and therefore it is necessary to say them very clearly. You will also need to help them to say addresses properly. The children will have heard these pronounced in a non-English way by other immigrants and they will tend to say them at a great speed. Make them slow down, put in proper stress and work on any problem sounds that may crop up. These are the first priorities, but you can then usefully practise names of English children in the school and perhaps the names of useful shops. Practice in pronouncing each other's addresses and the names of major roads and places in the neighbourhood is also essential. This can also be linked with practice in giving directions, e.g. *how can I get to* . . . from here?, and dialogues and pronunciation exercises can be adapted or extended to include relevant names. Include relevant names among the material you use in other pronunciation exercises.

---

9 The effect of reading on pronunciation

Phonic work is a necessary part of learning to read, and, to repeat, this kind of activity should not be used instead of speechwork. It is desirable that children should not meet the written word[1] until they have a good, oral acquaintance with the language and know what the words they read sound like and what they mean. They should also have a feel for the rhythm of English. Even then the children will often be caught out by spelling/pronunciation discrepancies. You may find yourself with a class of children who can read mechanically without understanding. This is usually because they have not had enough oral experience and they will be most confused by spelling and pronunciation. If you have children like this, try to put matters right by giving them lots of speechwork and oral work, letting them read only material which you know they will understand because you have been through it with them first orally. Remember particularly that the relationship between spelling and pronunciation is far more straightforward in all the main immigrant languages than it is in English, so the tendency to look to spelling for help in pronouncing will be even greater than it would otherwise be. Letters that are not pronounced, e.g. the *r* in *card*, will also be a pitfall.

---

10 Keeping a check on individual children

These areas of pronunciation work apply of course to all your children irrespective of their language origins or their level of English. When it comes to detail, be prepared for different difficulties from child to child, even where they have the same native language; they may speak different dialects, or they may have been exposed to different English accents and to different approaches to English teaching. (See page 7 for an explanation of how one's native language can interfere with

---

[1]Nevertheless, when the children are ready for reading, they will need help in relating sounds to spelling and you will find suggestions for this in SCOPE *Stage One*.

the learning of a new language.) Because of these differences, it is useful to keep a record chart, strictly for your own use, not for the classroom wall. A chart is more immediately visible than a card index, but if your class is very large and heterogeneous, a card index may be more practicable.

	Children's names	bat bet	ship sheep	not nought note	late let	rhythm and neutral vowel	Pin bin	wine vine
Greek								
Indian & Pakistani								
Difficulties								

An example of a record chart

To make a chart, use large squared paper and draw two axes. List the children's names along the left-hand vertical axis; group them according to language origin or according to the level of English, whichever is more to the point for your particular class. Along the bottom axis list the problems which arise. No child will have all the problems, fortunately, so in each child's row black out squares that do not represent problems. You should then find within each grouping of children that there are a good many common problems, and this in turn will facilitate organisation; you can attend to these children in groups, and you will not have to make other children waste time on irrelevant points. Gradually, as you observe progress on the different points, you can place a tick in the squares. These ticks will not mean you can forget about that problem for that child, but rather that you have both made

42

an initial impact on it and can turn more attention to other points.

You will find that the greatest differences between children's problems lie in the area of individual sounds and sound combinations. Rhythm and intonation will affect them all, and all the children will benefit from the same kind of rhythm and intonation work. Work on vowel contrasts is never a waste of time, but it is not a good idea to make a child practise, for the sake of the other children, say f and p, if this pair does not confuse him.

From time to time you will also meet a child whose difficulties are essentially of a psychological nature or who has a physical impediment. It may be that he has the same problem in speaking his first language.

PART TWO

1 First priority problems for the different language groups

This section gives a summary of the difficulties that are described and treated in detail in Part Two: **2**.

The difficulties of children from India and Pakistan have been treated collectively here. This is because the English pronunciation problems of learners speaking Hindi, Urdu, Gujerati and Punjabi are very similar; and differences between these groups are often no greater than differences within them caused by dialect variation. Many of the children speaking these languages will also have been used to hearing 'Indian English' spoken at home in India and Pakistan, and this has developed its own distinctive pronunciation system. Many children coming from remote areas speak very restricted and simplified versions of their own language; and this applies to grammar and vocabulary as well as pronunciation.

---

1 Indians and Pakistanis

Consonants

i WORDS BEGINNING WITH:

p and b	Refer to Section 2, page 52
t and d	57, 60
k and g	63

ii THE CONTRASTS:

f and v	68
w and v	70
f and p	67

iii THE CONTRASTS:

s ʃ z ʒ tʃ dʒ as in *sue shoe*   *zoo measure*   *catch cadge* ‹   72– 84

i The placing of stress in particular words.
(Word stress)

ii The stressing of words and syllables important
in a particular sentence. (Sentence stress)

iii The use of ə i u for words and syllables when not
stressed.

iv The even spacing of sentence stress.

v As much imitation of English speakers' intonation
as possible.

---

2   Italians

Consonants

48

Vowels

Rhythm and Intonation

---

3 Turkish Cypriots

Consonants

49

4 Greek Cypriots

Consonants

Vowels

2 Individual problems and practice material

Component sounds

This material should be used selectively. Do not attempt to work through all the exercises. You will find you only need some of the material offered for a particular problem and it is very important that you should use only words and patterns that are already familiar. To this end, you can also add examples to be more relevant to your children's needs, particularly relevant names. On pages 46–51 above you will find the problems of different language groups summarised; below there are explanations of how these practices should be used.

There is practice material at three different levels, A, B and C:

LEVEL A: for beginners. This is related specifically to the first five units of *Scope, Stage One*; the vocabulary and syntax are therefore very limited.

LEVEL B: for learners in their first year of English. This draws language from the whole of *Scope, Stage One*, but no other language is used.

LEVEL C: for older learners, especially those who have rather a rambling vocabulary but limited structural grasp.

Classes using levels B or C should also draw simple examples from level A, as by and large, the succeeding levels do not duplicate each other.

Consonants

1   p **as in** *pin*

Concerns: Indians and Pakistanis

Problem: confusing p and b, particularly at the beginning of words or at the beginning of stressed syllables as in *appear*.

Southern English adds a slight h sound (aspiration) to the p in these circumstances, and if you teach this – (p^h) –, it will help the child to make the p b distinction clearer. Whether or not you teach the p^h version, you must practise the p b contrast.

Ear training

DISTINGUISHING p AND b SOUNDS.

PRACTICE 1

LEVEL A   Pick out the p words:
pen ball book pencil pink boat putting bag

LEVEL B   Same/different practice.
beach peach bought port bill pill bark park

LEVEL C   Same/different practice:
*bunch punch bull pull bounce pounce bowl pole bin pin
back pack bet pet*

Production

i Words beginning with p.
To teach p^h, see that enough air is released with the p to make a light piece of paper flutter if held in front of the mouth.

PRACTICE 2

LEVEL A   Practise saying:
*pen pencil pink putting pint pullover pound past
piece paper pair*

LEVEL B   Practise saying:
*peach pullover put paper park pen parcel post
penny pound pocket*

LEVEL C   Practise saying:
*peach pack post policeman porter pancake point
piece pick pop pond penny purse pub pain pear
pan*

ii Contrasting p and b.

If you are teaching p^h, see the paper flutters for p but not for b. Use the material in PRACTICE 1 above.

iii Practising these in sentences.

Remember that we use p^h to begin stressed words or syllables where a vowel follows and otherwise we use a p with no h sound. How you choose to stress any sentence is, of course, up to you; but make sure the children are imitating your stressing. p is not aspirated when it occurs in clusters, as for example, in *sport*. More advanced children can be shown to use the p^h version when it comes right at the end of a sentence, as in *turn off the tap*. You do not want them to add a final vowel, but simply to release the breath just audibly.

PRACTICE 3

LEVEL A A piece of paper please.
Can I have a piece of paper please.
A pen and pencil please.
Can I have a pen and pencil please.
The pink pullover.
The pink pullover is mine.
A pair of plimsolls.
I've lost a pair of plimsolls.

LEVEL B A parcel from Pakistan.
The postman has got a parcel from Pakistan.
Playing in the park.
They're playing in the park.
A pound of plums.
He bought a pound of plums.
The big pen.
The biggest pen.
The biggest pen is in his pocket.
There's a penny.
There's a penny in my pocket.
Your pullover.
Put on your pullover.

LEVEL C Peaches, pears, bananas, plums.
Postman, baker, policeman, porter.
Put the pancake in the pan.
A penny in my purse.
Perhaps there's a penny in my purse.
The best programme.
Pick the best programme.
Pack and post this.
Pack and post this big parcel please.
If you prick a balloon it will pop.

54

2 b **in mid-position, as in** *rubber*

Concerns: Greek speakers

Problem: a tendency to pronounce words like *rubber* and *cabbage* as 'rumber' and 'cambage', putting an m before b when it occurs in a mid-word position. There is a similar problem with mid d which tends to become 'nd' and with mid g which tends to become 'ng-g'; thus you may hear 'lander' for *ladder*, and 'fong-gy' for *foggy*.

Ear training

Make the child listen very carefully to words like *rubber*, *ladder* and *foggy*. He may think he can hear m, n or ŋ at first.

Production

i. Words with b in mid-position, like *rubber*.

PRACTICE 4

LEVEL A Listen carefully and practise saying:
rubber   cabbage   table   cupboard   zebra

LEVEL B Listen carefully and practise saying:
label   rabbit   about   oblong   zebra

LEVEL C Listen carefully and practise saying:
robber   problem   probably   neighbour   able

ii. Check their ability to pronounce mid d as in *ladder*.

PRACTICE 5

LEVEL A Listen carefully and practise saying:
cloudy   radio   bedroom   reading

LEVEL B Listen carefully and practise saying:
headache   reading   ladybird   spider   sadder

LEVEL C Listen carefully and practise saying:
adding   ladder   hiding   riding   order   garden   anybody   bedroom   radio

iii. Check their ability to pronounce mid g as in *foggy*.

PRACTICE 6

LEVEL A Listen carefully and practise saying:
august   foggy   playground

LEVEL B Listen carefully and practise saying:
programme   bigger   segment   tiger   magazine

Listen carefully and practise saying:
figure   digging   luggage   baggage   cigarette   sugar

iv. Practise all these in sentences.

PRACTICE 2–7

LEVEL A   A cloudy day.
A cloudy day in August.
It's cloudy today.
x Where's Tony?
y He's in his bedroom.
x What's he doing in the bedroom?
y He's reading.

LEVEL B   A ladybird, a spider, a rabbit.
He's reading.
He's reading a magazine.
He's reading a magazine in the playground.

These sentences also contain words like *donkey* with the 'ng'
ŋ sound. Try these only when the children can say the first
sentences easily.

A zebra, a tiger, a donkey.
This programme is longer.
This programme is longer than that one.
The angry tiger.
The angry tiger roared.

LEVEL C   (This is a walkie-talkie report from a policeman watching a
burglar at work. There are also many words with mb, nd
and ng in this passage. These are marked with an asterisk
and the sentences containing them are marked in the same
way. Do not try these sentences until the children are saying
the other sentences easily.)

Mr Higgins, the nextdoor neighbour, is in his garden.

He's digging his cabbages.

*Now he's stuck his spade in the *ground and stopped work.

He's climbing over the fence into this garden.

*Now he has *found a ladder and has *leaned it against the
house.

*He's looking *around him, but he *can't see anybody.

Mr Higgins is probably a burglar. I'll wait and see what he
does.

*Yes, I thought so. He's climbing the ladder and opening the bedroom *window.

He's inside the bedroom now.

*My men are *surrounding the house, but Mr Higgins *can't see them.

*They're hiding in the *undergrowth and in the garden shed.

*Here he is, at the *window again.

*He's *found a radio and a silver sugar bowl. We were right. He is a burglar.

3.1   t **as in** *tin*

Concerns: Indians and Pakistanis

Problem: confusing t and d, particularly at the beginning of words or where t occurs at the beginning of a stressed syllable as in *return*. This is a problem similar to that described in (1) above for p, and the same techniques apply.

Ear training

DISTINGUISHING t AND d IN WORD LISTS AND PAIRS.

PRACTICE 8

LEVEL A   Pick out the t words:
two   tea   door   do   tie   dark   toes   tap   day   towel
Same/different practice:
two   do

LEVEL B   Same/different practice:
town   down

Pick out the t words:
*ten   top   dog   times   tell   duck   tin   donkey
town   tunnel*

LEVEL C   Same/different practice:
*tie die   tore door   ton done   trip drip   try dry   touch
Dutch*

Production

i. Words beginning with t.

PRACTICE 9

LEVEL A   Practise saying:
two   tea   tie   tap   toes   table   towel   time   television

C

57

Practise saying:
ten top tired times tell tin town tunnel two tea tiger ticket tall tights testing tongue temperature tablet

LEVEL C Practise saying:
tie take ton town touch taste taxi two ten turn terrible talk time

ii. Words with t at the beginning of their stressed syllable, as in *return*. See that the stressed syllable really stands out. Omit this step with beginners.

PRACTICE 10

LEVEL B Practise saying:
September October return potato

LEVEL C Practise saying:
attack detective guitar moustache hotel alternative pretend

iii. Practise t and d in lists and word pairs, using the material in PRACTICE 8 above.

iv. Practise these in sentences. Remember that t^h is used only at the beginning of words or syllables that are stressed.

PRACTICE 11

LEVEL A Two ties.
Two ties and a towel.
Tea-time.
It's dark at tea-time.
See the rhyme 'Clocks' on page 155.

LEVEL B A return ticket.
A return ticket to Teddington.
How much is a return ticket to Teddington?
A tin of tablets.
Two tins of tablets.
Take two tins of tablets.
Take two tins of tablets to Tony.
Take his temperature.
Take Tony's temperature.
Do you like sugar in your tea?
Two lumps or ten?

LEVEL C What's the time?
It's ten to two.
Please would you tell me the time?
Take a taxi.
Tony's taking a taxi.
Tony's taking a taxi to town.
Don't touch.
Don't touch the television.
A terrible hotel.
Tom stayed at a terrible hotel.
There was no water.
When he turned on the taps there was no water.
The tea tasted terrible too.

3.2 t as in *tin*

Concerns: Italian and Turkish speakers, and also Indians and Pakistanis, though these are more often affected by problem **3.3** below

Problem: forming t with the tongue-tip touching the upper teeth, which gives the speech a distinctly 'foreign' flavour, especially when combined with the problem **3.1** above. This is known as the 'dental' t. The English t is made with the tongue-tip touching the alveolar ridge. (See the diagram on page 19.)

Ear training

If you are able to demonstrate the 'dental' and the English t, do so, and let the children distinguish them in simple words, using PRACTICE 9 above. Otherwise, make the children listen very carefully to the way you say these words.

Production

i. Words beginning with t. To help you check whether the tongue is in the right position, try asking the child to make a slight s sound immediately after the t. This will encourage the tongue into the necessary position for English t. Use the material in PRACTICE 9 above.

ii. Words with t in a mid-position, like *return*. (LEVELS B and C only.) Use the material in PRACTICE 10 above.

iii. Practise these in sentences. Use the material in PRACTICE 11 above.

3.3   t **as in** *tin*

Concerns: Indians and Pakistanis

Problem: forming t with the tongue-tip bent back and touching the roof of the mouth much further back than in the English t sound. This is known as 'retroflexion', and the retroflex t, if used for English, gives a very strange effect, especially as it influences any surrounding vowel sounds.

Ear training

Demonstrate the differences between 'retroflex' t and the English sound, if you can, and let the children distinguish them. Use material from PRACTICE 9 above. If you cannot demonstrate the difference properly, simply get the children to listen very attentively to the English sound in simple words beginning with t. Use the material in PRACTICE 9 above.

Production

i. Words beginning with t. Use the material in PRACTICE 9, above.
ii. Words with t in a mid-position, like *return*. Use the material in PRACTICE 10 above (LEVELS B and C only)
iii. Practise these in sentences. Use the material in PRACTICE 11 above.

4.1   d **in mid-position, as in** *ladder*

Concerns: Greek speakers

Problem: a tendency to pronounce words like *ladder* as 'lander', putting a n sound before d when it occurs in mid-position. See problem **2** above.

4.2   d **as in** *din*

Concerns: Italian and Turkish speakers, also Indians and Pakistanis, although these are affected more often by problem **4.3** below

Problem: forming d with the tongue-tip touching the upper teeth, the 'dental' d. See the notes on 'dental' t in problem **3.2** above. The same techniques apply here.

Ear training

Demonstrate the difference between 'dental' and English d sounds if you can do so. Otherwise make the children listen and watch you very carefully, as you demonstrate the English sound. Let them experiment among themselves while you listen unobtrusively. Use the material in PRACTICE 12 below.

Production

i. Words beginning with d. It may help, as a temporary step to get the tongue in the right position, to ask the children to make a very slight z sound immediately after the d.

PRACTICE 12

LEVEL A Listen carefully and practise saying:
desk   door   dinner   drinking   down   drying   dates   dress   dried

LEVEL B Listen carefully and practise saying:
drawn   day   dark   dinner   dearer   doctor   don't   dangerous   dish   dirty   dig   donkey   duck   deliver   dad   dog   different

LEVEL C Listen carefully and practise saying:
dentist   do   doing   done   drive   December   daughter   deep   district   difficult   different   date   double   dare   dear   door   doctor   drive

ii. Words with d in a mid or final position, like *riding* or *ride*.

PRACTICE 13

LEVEL A Practise saying:
red   cloud   made   wind   child   reading   cloudy   windy   shoulder   window   good   cold   outside

LEVEL B Practise saying:
bird   played   had   stood   bend   second   painted   combed   garden   ladder   yesterday   headache   posted   delivered   collected   found

LEVEL C Practise saying:
hide   lid   bad   sound   child   filled   leading   sadder   understand   told   tried   surprised   good   road   need

iii. Practise these in sentences.

PRACTICE 14

LEVEL A   x Come here, David.

Y Yes, all right. I'm coming.

X It's dinner time.

Y Good. Ooh. It's cold outside!

X Shut the window and the door.

LEVEL B X Dad.

Y Hallo.

X There's a dog in the garden.

Y A dog?

X Yes, Dad. A black one.

Y Oh, I found one yesterday. Is it David's?

X No. This is a different one.

LEVEL C X Do you know a good doctor?

Y Yes, I do. Doctor Dodd in Bradford Road.

X Ah! Doctor Dodd. Thank you.

Y I need a dentist.

X Well, I go to Mr. Dyson in Derby Drive.

Y Tyson?

X No. Dyson, spelt with a D.

4.3 **d as in *din***

Concerns: Indians and Pakistanis

Problem: forming d with the tongue-tip bent back and touching the roof of the mouth much further back than in the English d. This is the 'retroflex' d. See the notes on 'retroflex' t in problem **3.3** above. The same procedures apply.

Ear training

Demonstrate the difference between 'retroflex' and English d sounds if you can. Otherwise make the children listen and watch you very carefully as you demonstrate the English sound. Let them experiment among themselves while you listen unobtrusively. Use the material in PRACTICE 12 above.

Production:

i. Words beginning with d. Use the material in PRACTICE 12 above.

ii. Words with d in mid or final position, like *riding* or *ride*. Use the material in PRACTICE 13 above.

iii. Practise these in sentences. Use the material in PRACTICE 14 above.

62

5.1 k **as in** *cot*

Concerns: Indians and Pakistanis

Problem: confusing k and g when they occur at the beginning of words or at the beginning of a stressed syllable as in o'clock. This is the same problem as described in **1** above for p, and the same procedures apply.

Ear training

DISTINGUISHING k AND g IN LISTS AND WORD PAIRS.

PRACTICE 15

LEVEL A Same/different practice:
curl girl

Pick out the k words:
car cup café girl green coat kerb give cabbage go

LEVEL B Same/different practice:
coat goat came game class glass

LEVEL C Same/different practice:
could good cold gold ankle angle

Production

i. Words beginning with k.

PRACTICE 16

LEVEL A Listen carefully and practise saying:
coat car cutting cold clock come cup café kerb cabbage

LEVEL B Listen carefully and practise saying:
cow catch kite cough cold coat came class cart coming

LEVEL C Listen carefully and practise saying:
can could climb colour call kill country cat canary crocodile keep kitchen

ii. Practise word pairs like *coat/goat*. Use the material in PRACTICE 15 above.

iii. Practise these in sentences. Remember that we use k^h only at the beginning of words or syllables that are stressed.

LEVEL A x Come here, Carol.
        y Coming!
        x Here's a cup of tea!
        y Thank you. Oh, Kate! It's cold!

LEVEL B x Where's Mr. Clark?
        y He's got a cold and a cough.
        x Is he coming to school today?
        y No. His cold is very bad.

LEVEL C x I think Carol likes animals.
        y Because she comes from the country?
        x Perhaps, – but she's got three cats, two canaries and a crocodile.
        y Where does she keep the crocodile?
        x In the kitchen.
        y In the kitchen!
        x Yes.– It's not a real one. It's made of wood.

5.2   k **as in** *cot*

Concerns: Greek speakers

Problem: making a slight j sound after k in words like *kick*, *came* and *cat*, where the vowel following is formed at the front of the mouth. See page 15 for a chart showing 'front' vowels.

Ear training

Make the children listen to you very carefully.

Production

i. Practise words like *cot* and *cool* with 'back' vowels where the child will not be tempted to say k^j.

PRACTICE 17

LEVEL A   Practise saying:
cup   come   coat   cupboard

LEVEL B   Practise saying:
calf   comb   cough   cold

LEVEL C   Practise saying:
cool   caught   course   could   cork   call   cook   cost

ii. Practise words like *kick* and *came* with 'front' vowels. The children will be tempted to say k^j with these words. Get them to use the kind of k sound they used with the words in the last practice.

LEVEL A Listen carefully and practise saying:
kerb café cabbage carrot scales carol Kate king's

LEVEL B Listen carefully and practise saying:
curtain can catch came chemist carry king

LEVEL C Listen carefully and practise saying:
*curl cat calendar key kill cake keep case kick
catch kitten*

iii. Practise in sentences.

PRACTICE 19

LEVEL A X Carol, where's Kate's Cafe?
Y In King's Road.
X Where's King's Road?
Y In Kentish Town.

LEVEL B X Where can I find a chemist?
Y Why do you want a chemist?
X Because I've got a cough.
Y Come with me. There's a chemist in King Street.
X Oh, thank you.
Y Can you carry my case/bag for me?
X Oh dear! Is it very far to the chemist's?

LEVEL C X Come and help me catch the kitten.
Y Which kitten?
X The one Kate found yesterday.
Y I can see it now. Under the car.
X Come here, Kitten!
Y It's playing with your key-case.

6.1 g **as in** *gate*

Concerns: Greek speakers

Problem: a tendency to say gʲ instead of g in words like *gill* and *gate*, where g is followed by a 'front' vowel. See page 15 for a chart showing 'front' vowels.

Ear training

Make the children listen to you very carefully.

Production:

i. Practise words like *good* and *go* with 'back' vowels. The children will use the right kind of g for these.

LEVEL A Practise saying:
good go going got

LEVEL B Practise saying:
goat fireguard ago gun

LEVEL C Practise saying:
*begun gourd goose god gold gone golf gorgeous
govern*

ii. Practise words like *give* and *get* with 'front' vowels following the g. Get the children to try to use the same kind of g they used for the last practice.

PRACTICE 21

LEVEL A Listen carefully and practise saying:
girl again gate altogether

LEVEL B Listen carefully and practise saying:
girl give get gallop together

LEVEL C Listen carefully and practise saying:
*geese game began begin gadget gas gay give
garage gave gallon*

iii. Practise these in sentences.

PRACTICE 22

LEVEL A The gate's open.
The gate's open again.
Carol's a girl.
Carol's a good girl.

LEVEL B The girls went home.
The girls went home together.
Please give me a cabbage.
Get some fruit.
Get some fruit for Mrs. Gale.

LEVEL C The old grey geese.
The old grey geese began to cackle.
This is a good game.
Six gallons please.
Give me six gallons please.
The garage gave me six gallons.
This is a gas-lighter.
This gadget is a gas-lighter.

6.2 g in mid-position as in *foggy*

Concerns: Greek speakers

Problem: a tendency to pronounce words like *foggy* as 'fong-gy', putting a ŋ sound before the g when it occurs in a mid-position. See problem 2 above.

7.1 f as in *fine*

Concerns: Indians and Pakistanis

Problem: using p instead of f, so that *foot* becomes *put*. This is especially likely in words which have entered their languages as loan words from English.

Ear training

DISTINGUISHING f AND p.

PRACTICE 23

LEVEL A   Same/different practice:
foot put   fare pair

LEVEL B   Same/different practice:
four paw   fork pork   fought port   fast past   fence pence

LEVEL C   Same/different practice:
fan pan   faint paint   fond pond   full pull   fill pill

Production

i. Practise words beginning with f. Draw attention to the upper teeth, which should be touching the lower lip, but lightly so that a little breath can pass through.

PRACTICE 24

LEVEL A   Practise saying:
*four   five   finished   fifty   flag   from   face   fork   foggy
feet   foot   fare*

LEVEL B   Practise saying:
*family   football   fence   fighting   floor   finger   four   fights
fought   fork   fast   field   *forward   fighter*

LEVEL C   Practise saying:
*fan   faint   fond   full   fill   film   finish   four   fifteen   before
phone   father   foggy   furious   forest   food   follow*

ii. Practise f and o in pairs like *foot/put*. Use the material in
PRACTICE 23 above.

iii. Practise these in sentences.

PRACTICE 25

LEVEL A
X What's the fare to Finchley?
Y From the station?
X No, from here. Is it fourpence?
Y No. Fivepence.

LEVEL B
X Did you see the football on telly?
Y Yes. My family likes football.
X Who was the fast *forward?
Y That was Freddy Foot.
X Oh, was it? My father says he's not a footballer, he's a fighter.
Y Why?
X Because he fights on the field.
*If necessary teach this use of the word *forward*, which the course does not
introduce.

LEVEL C
X What time does the film finish?
Y It finishes at four fifteen.
X Before the next film begins, I must go and phone my father.*
Y Why must you phone him?
*Let x invent a reason each time the dialogue is said.

7.2 f **as in** *fine* **and** v **as in** *vine*

Concerns: Indians and Pakistanis

Problem: confusion between f and v.

Ear training

DISTINGUISHING f AND v IN WORD PAIRS AND LISTS.

PRACTICE 26

LEVEL A
Pick out the f words. Then repeat, picking out the v words:
*four   of fifty   halves   half   very   foot   have   haven't
full   eleven   vest   pullover*

LEVEL B
Same/different practice:
leaf leave

Pick out the f words. Then repeat, picking out the v words:
*leaf   fight   leaves   frightened   afternoon   favourite   film
give   heavy   fire   paraffin   move   village*

Same/different practice:
fine vine   fail veil   half halve   relief relieve

Production

i. Practise words like *foot*, beginning with f. Let the children feel their larynxes. They should be able to feel vibration for v, but none for f.

PRACTICE 27

LEVEL A Practise saying:
*fur   furry   foggy   fork   finished   four   fifty   foot   feet
full   flag   from   after   café   knife   half   five*

LEVEL B Practise saying:
*first   find   found   finger   fight   flying   frightened   floor
favourite   frying-pan   cupful   teaspoonful   afternoon   left
half   leaf   scarf   cliff · fire   foot   fast   sofa   shelf*

LEVEL C Practise saying:
*film   fine   fix   fold   fight   fail   finish   safe   fact   face
before   afternoon   alphabet   telephone   knife   life   half
laugh   relief   free*

ii. Practise word lists and pairs with f and v. Use the material in
PRACTICE 26 above.

iii. Practise these in sentences.

PRACTICE 28

LEVEL A Five vests.
Four pullovers.
Five vests and four pullovers.
Have you got four feet?
No, I haven't.
A knife and fork.
Can I have a knife and fork please.

LEVEL B Do firemen go on foot?
Do firemen go on foot to a fire?
No, in a fire engine.
They go in a fire engine.
When a house is on fire, they go in a fire engine.
They must move fast.
They must move fast, or they arrive too late.

X I've lost my favourite scarf.
Y Is it on the floor?

X No, it isn't.
Y Is it on the sofa?
X No, it isn't. Ah – here it is. I've found it!
Y Where was it?
X On the shelf in the cupboard.

LEVEL C X Are you free this afternoon?
Y Yes, I think so, if I can finish this job first.
X Would you like to see that film, *'........'?
Y Yes. Fine! I'd love to see it.
*Let the children suggest or invent film titles.

---

8 v **as in** *vine* **and** w **as in** *wine*
Concerns: Indians, Pakistanis, Turkish and Greek speakers

Problem: confusion between v and w, or the use of a compromise half-and-half sound for both.

Ear training

DISTINGUISHING V AND W.

PRACTICE 29

LEVEL A Pick out the w words. Then repeat, picking out the v words:
*wall vest pullover of what where went vegetable
weight wet five windy seven one have white woman
very*

LEVEL B Pick out the w words. Then repeat, picking out the v words:
*water walk why halves give stove work move village
west valley twist whiskers deliver away*

LEVEL C Same/different practice:
wine vine wet vet wheel veal while vile

Production

i. Practise words with v. Point out that the top teeth and lower lip should come together.

PRACTICE 30

LEVEL A Practise saying:
*vest very vegetable pullover five seven have of
television lavatory eleven seventy evening*

LEVEL B Practise saying:
*village valley van move stove give every heavy
halves deliver never reserve*

70

Practise saying:

vine   vet   veal   vile   vote   voter   vaccinate   verse   value valuable   shelves   knives   live   lives   leave   leaves   love loves   serve   serves   service   travel   travels   traveller   sieve brave   velvet

ii. Practise words with w. Point out that only the lips, and not the teeth, come close together. If they come too close, the sound will have too much friction, and may for that reason sound too much like v. An alternative way of teaching w is to treat it as the vowel sound u as in *good*, which requires the lips to be in the same position as for w.

PRACTICE 31

LEVEL A   Practise saying:

wall   what   where   went   weight   wet   windy   one   white woman   washing   with   walking   window   was

LEVEL B   Practise saying:

water   walk   why   when   work   west   twist   away   whiskers once   twice   warm   wellingtons   wore   wearing   what   we

LEVEL C   Practise saying:

wine   wet   wheel   while   were   will   won't   want   would world   wish   watch   win   wore   wise   ways   wire   wedding week   well   worth   winter   wool   wood   welcome   where was

iii. Practise lists or word pairs with *w* and *v*. Use the material in PRACTICE 29 above.

iv. Practise these in sentences.

PRACTICE 32

LEVEL A   X   What's on television this evening?
         Y   Where's the TV Times?
         X   Here it is, by the window.
         Y   What is on? Er. – This evening it's . . . .*
         *Let Y suggest or invent a programme.

LEVEL B   X   What's wrong?
         Y   This van is in front of my car, and I can't move.
         X   We must move the van then.
         Y   Move it! It's too heavy!
         X   No, it isn't. Come on! One, two, three, – *heave!
         * Heave is a new word. Teach it before you start practising the dialogue.

LEVEL C   X   I've lost my watch.
         Y   Where did you lose it?

X In Liverpool yesterday, I think.
Y Was it valuable?
X It was worth twenty-five pounds.
Y Guess what!
X What?
Y *I found* a watch in Liverpool yesterday!

9.1 s **as in** *sip*

Concerns: Indians, Pakistanis and Greek speakers

Problem: Confusing s as in *sip* and ʃ as in *ship*. See problem 11 below.

9.2 s **as in** *cats*

Concerns: Indians and Pakistanis especially

Problem: failing to pronounce s at the end of plural words like *cats* or verb forms like *likes,* or to mark possession as in *Mike's*. This is not solely a pronunciation problem, but the awkwardness of pronouncing it is one factor behind its frequent omission.

Ear training

DISTINGUISHING WORDS WITH AND WITHOUT AN s ENDING, (like *cat/cats*).

This should not be difficult, but it is an essential step in focusing attention on the final s.

PRACTICE 33

LEVEL A Same/different practice:
date dates   nut nuts   carrot carrots   grape grapes   lollipop lollipops

LEVEL B Same/different practice:
rabbit rabbits   snake snakes   elephant elephants   giraffe giraffes   like likes   bite bites   peck pecks   sit sits   sleep sleeps   *Mark Mark's   Pat Pat's
*Mark/Mark's substitute names relevant to your class. Choose examples that end with a t, p, or a k.

LEVEL C Same/different practice:
hat hats   coat coats   sock socks   shirt shirts   belt belts mac macs   boot boots   get gets   want wants   stop stops

make makes   hope hopes   drop drops   work works
*Jack Jack's   Kate Kate's
*Substitute names relevant to your class. Choose examples that end with a
t, p or a k.

Production
i. Practise words ending with a vowel and s, like *horse*. This
should also be quite easy.

PRACTICE 34

LEVEL A   Practise saying:
this   cross   face   bus   dress   Cyprus   class   house

LEVEL B   Practise saying:
twice   grass   space   nurse   chase   mouse   us   rice

LEVEL C   Practise saying:
*horse   miss   fuss   loose   boss   loss   glass   course   purse
worse*

ii. Practise words ending with a consonant and s, like *cats*, *likes*
and *Pat's*. If necessary, split them up: *cat – s*. Repeat each word,
gradually reducing the gap until the two parts merge into one
word. While practising you can exaggerate the s, but finally it
need be only a rather slight sound. Better to overdo it, however,
than to leave it off.

PRACTICE 35

LEVEL A   Practise saying:
carrots   grapes   lollipops   dates   nuts   months   belts   vests

LEVEL B   Practise saying:
*rabbits   snakes   giraffes   elephants   cups   plates   forks
stripes   spots   likes   bites   pecks   sits   sleeps   box
wasps   cakes   *Mark's   Pat's*
*Substitute relevant names, choosing ones that end with p, t, or k.

LEVEL C   Practise saying:
*hats   coats   socks   shirts   belts   macs   boots   gets   wants
stops   makes   hopes   drops   works   *Jack's   Kate's*
*Substitute relevant names, choosing ones that end with p, or t or k

iii. Practise pairs of words like *cat/cats*. Use the material in
PRACTICE 33 above.

iv. Practise in sentences.

PRACTICE 36

LEVEL A   Some nuts.
Can I have some nuts, please.

73

Dates.
These are dates.
The grapes.
Where are the grapes?
Any nuts?
Have you got any nuts?
The lollipops.
The lollipops are on the table.

LEVEL B Some rabbits.
Tony saw some rabbits.
Two snakes.
He's got two snakes in a box.
Wasps sting.
Wasps sting when they are frightened.
Kate's brother.
Kate's brother likes cakes.

LEVEL C Big hats.
They wore big hats.
Warm coats.
They wore big hats and warm coats.
Thick socks.
They wore big hats, warm coats and thick socks.
Cheap macs.
She gets cheap macs.
Expensive boots.
She gets cheap macs but expensive boots.
Jack's shirts.
Those are Jack's shirts.

10.1 z **as in** *dogs*

Concerns: Indians and Pakistanis especially, and sometimes
Greek speakers and Italians

Problem: failing to pronounce z at the end of plural words like
dogs, verb forms like *comes* or to mark possession as in *Fred's*.
Alternatively, z may be replaced by s. The awkwardness of
pronouncing it is one of the various factors responsible for its
frequent omission.

Ear training

DISTINGUISHING WORDS WITH AND WITHOUT A z ENDING (like *dog/*
dogs). This should not be difficult.

PRACTICE 37

LEVEL A   Same/different practice:
chair chairs   door doors   cupboard cupboards
classroom classrooms   table tables   pen pens

LEVEL B   Same/different practice:
letter letters   brother brothers   van vans   parcel parcels
deliver delivers   need needs   give gives   run runs   *Mary
Mary's   Tony Tony's   Carol Carol's   Jim Jim's

*Substitute relevant names, choosing examples that end in vowels or 'voiced'
consonants (see page 18 for a list of 'voiced' consonants).

LEVEL C   Same/different practice:
car cars   train trains   plane planes   bicycle bicycles
ride rides   drive drives   go goes   run runs   *Bill Bill's
Joe Joe's   Jane Jane's   Fred Fred's

*Choose relevant names, ending in vowels or 'voiced' consonants (see page
18 for a list of 'voiced' consonants).

Production

i. Practise words ending with a vowel and z, like *days*. This
should not be hard.

PRACTICE 38

LEVEL A   Practise saying:
please   these   his   trees   peas   hours   was   is   nose
numbers   boys   blouse   shoes   ties   sisters   brothers   stairs
upstairs   Tony's   chairs   doors   tables

LEVEL B   Practise saying:
cars   days   these   those   eyes   ears   says   fires   has   does
carries   rises   changes   catches   Tony's   letters   Mary's
delivers   brothers   buys   sisters

LEVEL C   Practise saying:
cars   goes   Joe's   ways   sees   hears   fears   lose
excuse(vb.)   brothers   sisters   fathers   borrows   throws
careers   courses   factories   Peter's   flies   says

ii. Practise words ending with a consonant and z, like *dogs*,
reads and *Carol's*. If necessary, split them up to begin with into
dog – s, *read – s*, etc. Repeat each word several times, gradually
reducing the gap until the two parts merge into one word.

PRACTICE 39

LEVEL A   Practise saying:
cupboards   classrooms   schools   crayons   pens   pencils
trains   planes   girls   Carol's

Practise saying:
postcards parcels forms vans needs sells reads
telephones Jim's films mountains guns climbs gives
runs cards

Practise saying:
trains planes rides drives runs Jane's Fred's
machines jobs customs stations platforms comes mends
cleans travels means leaves arrives sales towns firms
times sons Jones

iii. Practise words pairs like *dog/dogs*. Use the material in
PRACTICE 38 above.

iv. Practise in sentences. These examples also involve s endings,
so see Problem **9.2** first if necessary.

PRACTICE 40

(The situation is moving furniture about the school. Y is the
Teacher directing operations.)

X These tables are from Room Two.
Y Please put them in the classrooms upstairs.
X Tony's got two chairs. Oh – here he is.
Y Good. Thank you Tony. Please put your chairs upstairs too.

The postman collects or delivers letters.
Tony's got three parcels and two letters.
These are his brothers and sisters.
Mr. Jones has two vans and three cars.
The cow gives milk, butter and cheese.
The giraffe doesn't jump; it runs.
John's letters.
Mary's cards.
Tony's ears.
Carol's eyes.

Mr. Jones is a salesman.
He sells machines to factories.
He drives the firm's car.
He travels to many towns.
Sometimes he goes by train.
Sometimes he drives the car.
Peter's brothers.
Susan's sisters.
Mr. Jones' sons.
His train arrives soon.

He flies jet aeroplanes.
He means what he says.

10.2 z as in *shoes*

Concerns: some Indians and Pakistanis

Problem: substituting dʒ as in *cadge* for z. dz as in *reads*, may also be substituted.

Ear training

DISTINGUISHING z AS IN *has*: dʒ AS IN *cadge*: dz AS IN *reads*.

PRACTICE 41

LEVEL A
1. Pick out the z words, like *his*
2. Repeat, picking out the dʒ words, like *change*
3. Repeat, picking out the dz words, like *beds*.
   chairs z *beds* dz *trains* z *his* z *shoes* z *change* dʒ
   pounds dz *jump* dʒ *zebra* z *jersey* dʒ *jacket* dʒ *zip* z

LEVEL B
1. Pick out the z words, like *says*
2. Repeat, picking out the dʒ words, like *bridge*
3. Repeat, picking out the dz words, like *birds*
   birds dz *says* z *bridge* dʒ *slides* dz *village* dʒ *means* z
   builds dz *jumps* dʒ *gentle* dʒ *zebra* z *giraffe* dʒ

LEVEL C
1. Pick out the z words, like *has*
2. Repeat, picking out the dʒ words, like *fridge*
3. Repeat, picking out the dz words, like *reads*
   has z *is* z *fridge* dʒ *judge* dʒ and dʒ *reads* dz *ways* z
   hedge dʒ *goes* z *needs* dz *ridge* dʒ *region* dʒ *badge* dʒ
   hers z *large* dʒ *page* dʒ *John* dʒ *zoo* z *zone* z *June* dʒ
   July dʒ *zigzag* z and z *zero* z

Production

i. Practise words with dʒ *as in cadge*.

PRACTICE 42

LEVEL A
Practise saying:
change

LEVEL B
Practise saying:
bridge village hedge

Practise saying:
fridge judge ridge badge large page June

ii. Practise words with z.

PRACTICE 43

LEVEL A Practise saying:
chairs his is please these cars boys trees

LEVEL B Practise saying:
was rose flowers peas quarters hours shoes says these does lives

LEVEL C Practise saying:
has does whose sees goes is ways hers zebra zoo zero sows

iii. Practise words with dz, like *heads*

PRACTICE 44

LEVEL A Practise saying:
beds pounds roads clouds yards

LEVEL B Practise saying:
birds sheds fields cards slides builds bends folds

LEVEL C Practise saying:
reads needs leads finds skids feeds seeds lids trades lads loads fields

iv. Practise these in sentences.

PRACTICE 45

LEVEL A x Eight yards please.
y Nine yards . . . . .
x No! *Eight* yards please.
y That's two pounds.
x Two *pounds*!

LEVEL B x Whose fields are these?
y They're Mr. White's.
x His hedges are good.
y Yes, he's a good farmer.
x Does he live in the village?
y No, he lives in the farmhouse near the bridge.
x Are those his sheds?
y No, those are Mr. Green's.

LEVEL C John goes to New Zealand in June.
Joe saw a zebra at the zoo.
The zebra feeds on grass.
Zero isn't one; it's nought.

11 ʃ as in *ship*

Concerns: Indians, Pakistanis and Greek speakers

Problem: confusing ʃ as in *ship* and s. The most usual
confusion is to replace ʃ with s, although there may be a
tendency among some Indian speakers to use ʃ for s in words
like *soon* where a lip-rounded vowel follows. (See page 14 for
a list of lip-rounded vowels.)

Ear training

DISTINGUISHING ʃ AND s IN PAIRS LIKE *shoe/sue* AND IN WORD
LISTS.

PRACTICE 46

LEVEL A Pick out the ʃ words, like *shoe*:
shoe six seven **she shop** same **shilling** saw sunny
soft **shirt**

LEVEL B Same/different practice:
sow show sign shine see she said shed

LEVEL C Same/different practice:
*sue shoe seat sheet sip ship *suit shoot sort short sock
shock save shave sell shell
*If, in your own speech, these are not minimal pairs, do not use these for this
exercise.

Production

i. Practise words like *shoe* with ʃ. Greeks will tend to use s.
Encourage them to protrude their lips, even though this is not
strictly necessary and to draw back the tip of the tongue a
little, letting the sound come out rather 'lazily'.

PRACTICE 47

LEVEL A Practise saying:
shoe she shop shilling shirt shiny shoulder

LEVEL B Practise saying:
show shine she shed shout shy

Practise saying:
shoe   sheet   sure   ship   shoot   short   shock   shave   shell
show

ii. Practise words with s.

PRACTICE 48
LEVEL A   Practise saying:
six   seven   same   saw   sunny   soft   sitting   sock   socks
some   sister   silk
LEVEL B   Practise saying:
sow   see   said   sign   sky   star   seat   sister   scarf
LEVEL C   Practise saying:
sue   seat   score   sip   suit   sort   sock   save   sell   such
sun   see

iii. Practise lists or pairs of words with ʃ and s like *ship/sip*.
Use the material in PRACTICE 46 above.

iv. Practise in sentences.

PRACTICE 49
LEVEL A   (Y is the sort of person who must always go one better.)
x   She saw some shirts at the shops.
y   Some shirts? *I* saw some shoes.
x   My sister bought a silk shirt.
y   *I* bought some shoes.

LEVEL B   Show me the cow sheds.
Why is she shouting?
The sun is shining.
She said sorry.

LEVEL C   x   May I try on this suit please?
y   Yes. Let me show you a changing-room.
x   Oh dear. This suit is too short.
y   Are you sure?
x   Can't you see how short it is?

12.1   ʒ **as in** *measure*

Concerns: Indians, Pakistanis, Greek and Italian speakers
(C level students only)

Problem: making ʒ as in *measure* sound like z or even, with some Indians and Pakistanis, like ʃ as in *ship*. This sound occurs in only a few words, but it is a difficulty. Practise it when you come across it.

Ear training

DISTINGUISHING ʒ WORDS.

PRACTICE 50

LEVEL A Pick out the words with ʒ like *measure*:
measure   Russia   leisure   treasure   razor   reason   fresher pleasure

Production

i. Practise words with ʒ like *measure*, as they arise in language work.

PRACTICE 51

LEVEL C Practise saying:
measure   leisure   treasure   pleasure

ii. Practise lists of words, contrasting ʒ with z, and with ʃ as in *ship*.

PRACTICE 52

LEVEL C x I went to Russia last year.
         y For what reason?
         x Business and pleasure.
         y Business and pleasure! You're lucky!

12.2   ʒ **as in** *measure*

Concerns: Turkish and some Italian speakers (C level students only)

Problem: making ʒ sound like dʒ, so that *leisure* becomes *ledger*.

Ear training

IDENTIFYING ʒ IN WORD LISTS.
PRACTICE 53

LEVEL C Pick out the words with ʒ :
measure   ledger   pleasure   dredger   leisure   treasure   lodger

Production

i. Practise words with ʒ. Point out that ʒ is only a 'voiced' version of ʃ as in *ship*. Try making a continuous ʃ sound: 'shhhh . . . .' and then adding a musical note to it. The result should be ʒ.
Use the material in PRACTICE 51 above.

ii. Practise word lists with words like *measure* with ʒ and words like *ledg*er with dʒ. Use the material in PRACTICE 53 above.

iii. Practise these in sentences.

PRACTICE 54

LEVEL C   My lodger has lots of leisure.
Can you judge the value of the treasures?
With pleasure!
Let's measure the shortest one.
I can see a small ship and a large dredger in the canal.

---

13   tʃ **as in** *chip*

Concerns: Indians, Pakistanis and Greek speakers

Problem: difficulty with tʃ as in *chip*, and possible confusion with dʒ as in *jug*, ʃ as in *ship* or ts as in *cats*.

Ear training

i. DISTINGUISHING tʃ AND dʒ IN LISTS OR WORD PAIRS LIKE *catch/cadge*.

PRACTICE 55

LEVEL A   Pick out the tʃ words:
child   jump   jersey   chimney   children   jacket

LEVEL B   Pick out the tʃ words:
church   pouch   pigeon   gentle   much   march   catch

LEVEL C   Same/different practice:
rich ridge   catch cadge   March marge   larch large

ii. DISTINGUISHING tʃ AND ʃ IN LISTS OF PAIRS LIKE *chips/ship*.

PRACTICE 56

LEVEL A   Pick out the tʃ words:
children   shoe   shirt   shop   change   chimney

82

Pick out the tʃ words:
chew *show* *chase* *shy* *chick* *cheese*

LEVEL C Same/different practice:
chip ship *chin shin* *cheap sheep* *chew shoe*

iii. DISTINGUISHING tʃ AND ts IN LISTS OR WORD PAIRS.

PRACTICE 57

LEVEL A Pick out the tʃ words:
each *hats* *much* *bunch* *dates* *pints*

LEVEL B Same/different practice:
catch cats *each eats*

LEVEL C Same/different practice:
match mats *porch ports* *hatch hats* *coach coats*

Production

i. Practise words with tʃ like *chip*.

PRACTICE 58

LEVEL A Practise saying:
child *children* *chimney* *change* *much* *each* *bunch*

LEVEL B Practise saying:
chew *chase* *chick* *cheese* *church* *pouch* *much* *scratch*
children

LEVEL C Practise saying:
chip *chin* *cheap* *China* *Chinese* *charm* *chat* *chalk*
chance *chap* *rich* *catch* *porch* *hatch* *coach* *match*
beach *brooch*

ii. Practice words with tʃ like *chip* in contrast to words with ʃ
like *ship*. Use the material in PRACTICE 56 above.

iii. Practice words with tʃ in contrast to words with dʒ, like
chip and *jump* respectively. Use the material in PRACTICE 55
above.

iv. Practise words with tʃ and ts, like *catch* and *cats*
respectively. Use the material in PRACTICE 57 above.

v. Practise in sentences.

PRACTICE 59

LEVEL A X How much are the dates?
Y Not much. Two shillings.
X Can I have some dates and a bunch of flowers please.

83

Y They're three shillings each. (X produces a pound note.)
Oh dear!
X What's wrong?
Y That's a pound note. Have you got any change?
X No, I'm sorry.

LEVEL B X I like cats very much. They're gentle animals.
Y *I* don't. They aren't very gentle with birds and mice.
X No, but they *are* gentle with children.
Y Gentle! They scratch, pounce and bite. That's not gentle!
X I must show you mine.

LEVEL C They left their coats in the coach.
These cheap pots are chipped.
The shepherd had to catch the sheep.
She has a chance of going to China.
I have just been having a chat with a chap on the beach.

---

14 dʒ **as in** *jug*

Concerns: Indians and Pakistanis, and Greek speakers

Problem: difficulty with dʒ and possible confusion with tʃ as in *catch* or with dz as in *lids*.

Ear training

i. DISTINGUISHING dʒ AND tʃ IN WORD PAIRS OR LISTS, e.g. *cadge* and *catch*. Use the material in PRACTICE 55 above.

ii. DISTINGUISHING dʒ AND dz IN LISTS OR WORD PAIRS LIKE *cadge/cads*. (LEVEL B and C only)

PRACTICE 60

LEVEL B Same/different practice:
hedge heads

Pick out the dʒ words:
hedge bridge change reads heads gentle giraffe birds

LEVEL C Same/different practice:
cadge cads budge buds siege seeds

Production

i. Practise words with dʒ like *jug*. If there is confusion with tʃ as in *catch*, try singing it on a musical note; the 'voicing' should convert it to dʒ.

84

PRACTICE 61

LEVEL A Practise saying:
jump   jacket   jersey   change

LEVEL B Practise saying:
gentle   pigeon   village   bridge

LEVEL C Practise saying:
*fridge   judge   large   ridge   barge   region   John   Jane
January   June   July   generally*

ii. Practise word pairs with dʒ and dz like *cadge* and *cads*.
(LEVELS B and C only.) Use the material in PRACTICE 60 above.

iii. Practise lists and word pairs like *cadge* and *catch* with dʒ
and tʃ. Use the material in PRACTICE 55 above.

iv. Practise these in sentences.

PRACTICE 62

LEVEL A Change your jacket.
How much is this jersey?
This jersey is two pounds ten.
One, two, three – jump!

LEVEL B X Which birds did you see?
Y Pigeons and blackbirds.
X Where were the pigeons?
Y In the fields.
X Where were the blackbirds?
Y In the hedges.

LEVEL C The four children's birthdays are in January, March, June and
July.
In which region of England is Leeds?
John got too much change.
They charged him too much.

15.1   θ **as in** *thin*

Concerns: Indians and Pakistanis. Turkish and Italian speakers
may be misled by the spelling, but see **15.2** below for their
more usual problem.

Ear training

i. DISTINGUISHING θ AND t, AS IN *thin* AND *tin*.

PRACTICE 63

LEVEL A Pick out the θ words:
thank you *tap* *three* *two* *twelve* *thirteen* *thumb* *tree*
tie

Same/different practice:
three tree

LEVEL B Pick out the θ words:
thin *thick* *tie* *two* *tell*

Same/different practice:
thick tick

LEVEL C Same/different practice:
thank tank *thought taught* *theme team*

ii. DISTINGUISHING θ AND d, AS IN *thin*/*din*.

PRACTICE 64

LEVEL A Pick out the θ words:
three *dried* *thumb* *thirty* *door* *day*

LEVEL B Same/different practice:
thick Dick *thirty dirty*

LEVEL C Same/different practice:
thumb dumb *thaw door* *thrill drill*

iii. DISTINGUISHING θ AND ð AS IN *thin*/*this*, IN WORD LISTS.

PRACTICE 65

LEVEL A Pick out the θ words:
thank *three* *Thursday* *this* *that* *they*

LEVEL B Pick out the θ words:
thirsty *these* *then* *three* *there*

LEVEL C Pick out the θ words:
thorn *those* *thus* *than* *think* *third* *with* *both* *bath*
path *loathe*

Production

i. Practise words with θ like *thin*. Initial teaching of this sound
is relatively simple because you can see what the speaker's
tongue and teeth are doing. Make the child put the tip of his
tongue between his teeth, to pronounce this sound. Once
he has learned to do this, he can learn to produce the same
effect but keeping his tongue out of sight.

LEVEL A   Practise saying:
thank you   three   thirteen   thumb   thirty   Thursday

LEVEL B   Practise saying:
thin   thick   thirsty   three hundred and thirty-three   thumb

LEVEL C   Practise saying:
*thought   theme   thaw   thrill   thorn   think   third   both
bath   path   Thursday   theatre   fourth*

ii. Practise θ and t in word pairs like *thin/tin* or lists. Use the material in PRACTICE 63 above.

iii. Practise θ and d in lists or word pairs like *thin/din*. Use the material in PRACTICE 64 above.

iv. Practise θ and $\eth$ as in *thin/then* in lists of words. Use the material in PRACTICE 65 above.

v. Practise these in sentences.

PRACTICE 67

LEVEL A   What are three thirteens?
They're thirty-nine.
Thank you.
Is today Thursday?
What are they doing?
These trees.
These three trees.
These three trees are the same.

LEVEL B   x Father, I'm thirsty.
           y I'm thirsty too. Let's sit down here and have a drink.
           x Have we got any tea?
           y Yes, here you are.
           x Thank you. That's better!

LEVEL C   x What's the date today?
           y I think it's Thursday the third.
           x I thought it was the fourth.
           y Tomorrow is the fourth, so today must be the third.

15.2 θ as in *thin*

Concerns: Turkish and Italian speakers

Problem: confusing θ with s, so that *thin* becomes *sin*.

Ear training

PRACTICE 68

LEVEL A   Pick out the θ words:
three   *see*   *six*   *soap*   **thank you**   **thumb**

LEVEL B   Pick out the θ words:
thin   **thick**   *sofa*   **Thursday**   *Sunday*   *sore*   *thirty*

Same/different practice:
think sink

LEVEL C   Same/different practice:
thick sick   *thaw saw*   *theme seem*   *thought sort*

Production

i. Practise words with θ like *thin*. Let the children put the tip of their tongues between their teeth when initially learning this sound. Later on they can keep the tongue out of sight. Use the material in PRACTICE 66 above.

ii. Practise lists and word pairs like *thin/sin* with θ and s. Use the material in PRACTICE 68 above.

iii. Practise these in sentences.

PRACTICE 69

LEVEL A   Three bars of soap please.
I can see thirty buses.
Here's the soap.
Thank you.

LEVEL B   She saw thick ice and snow.
See me at three thirteen.
See me at three thirteen on Sunday.
Six seventeen on Thursday.
See me at six seventeen on Thursday.
He's got a sore thumb.
Sit on the sofa.

LEVEL C   I thought she was sick.
She seemed a little unwell.
The thick snow started to thaw.
The theme was the theatre.

16.1 ð as in *this*

Concerns: Indians and Pakistanis. Italian and Turkish speakers may be misled by spelling, but see (**16.2**) below for their more usual problem.

Problem: general difficulty with ð, and possible confusion with d or with θ as in *thin*.

Ear training

i. DISTINGUISHING ð AND d AS IN ***those/doze.***

PRACTICE 70

LEVEL A   Pick out the ð words:
    they this that then did doesn't this
    Same/different practice:
    they day

LEVEL B   Pick out the ð words:
    the door than then did doesn't this
    Same/different practice:
    they day

LEVEL C   Same/different practice:
    then den their dare though doe

    ii. DISTINGUISHING ð AND θ IN WORD LISTS, e.g. *this/thin.* Use the material in PRACTICE 65 above.

Production

i. Practise words with ð like *this*. Let the children put the tips of their tongues between their teeth, or if they can already produce θ as in *thin*, get them to sing it on a continuous note. This should produce ð.

PRACTICE 71

LEVEL A   Practise saying:
    these they're this that mother brother father

LEVEL B   Practise saying:
    there than then this they that those father

LEVEL C   Practise saying:
    then theirs though those rather loathe other they're that

D

iv. Practise ð and d in lists and pairs, like *they/day*. Use the material in PRACTICE 70 above.

v. Practise ð and θ in lists, e.g. *this/thin*. Use the material in PRACTICE 65 above.

vi. Practise in sentences.

PRACTICE 72

LEVEL A
These are desks.
They're policemen.
This is Thursday.
This is the date.
Don't do that.

LEVEL B
They didn't think that.
There's the door.
It's thicker than that.
Didn't they thank you?
Those are Father's.

LEVEL C
Dared they think that?
These are their dogs.
Then they thanked Mr. Dixon.
They're in the third division.

16.2   ð as in *with*

Concerns: Turkish and Italian speakers

Problem: confusing ð and z, so that *with* becomes *wizz*.

Ear training

DISTINGUISHING ð AND z IN LISTS OF WORDS LIKE *with* AND *his*.

PRACTICE 73

LEVEL A
Pick out the ð words:
this   zebra   zip   that   who's   with

LEVEL B
Pick out the ð words:
*then   zebra   zip   than   feather   leather   mother   rising
brother   father*

LEVEL C
Pick out the ð words:
*than   zoo   zone   this   rather   lazy   razor   mother   cousin
reason   crazy   further   fizzy*

90

Production

i. Practise words with ð like *this*. If the children can now manage θ as in *thin*, get them to sing it on a sustained note. The result should be ð. Use the material in PRACTICE 71 above.

ii. Practise ð and z words like *with* and *his* in lists. Use the material in PRACTICE 73 above.

iii. Practise these in sentences. Use the material in PRACTICE 72 above.

---

17   ŋ **as in** *sung*

Concerns: Greek, Turkish and Italian speakers

Problem: pronouncing ŋ as 'ng-g', making *singer* into 'sing-ger', which is acceptable in some parts of England. If it is acceptable in your region, then naturally, do not treat this as a problem. Alternatively, you may hear k added when ŋ occurs at the end of a word, making *long* into 'long-k'; this applies particularly to Greeks.

Ear training

DISTINGUISHING WORDS LIKE *think/thing*. (LEVEL C only)

PRACTICE 74

LEVEL C   Same/different practice:
think thing   sink sing   rank rang   hunk hung   bank bang

Production

i. Practise words with ŋ followed by g as in *finger* and words like *thank* with ŋ followed by k.

PRACTICE 75

LEVEL A   Practise saying:
thank you   uncle   finger   triangle   rectangle

LEVEL B   Practise saying:
monkey   donkey   hungry   longer

ii. Practise words ending with ŋ, like *hung*. Children who can say *hunger* can practise such words in two parts, *hung–ger*, and then drop the second part, leaving simply *hung*. (LEVELS B and C only).

LEVEL B Practise saying:
*long swing along sing sting string

LEVEL C Practise saying:
*hung thing sing rang among bang ring bring
wing song
*These can be practised first on longer words: longer and hunger, then cut
off after ŋ.

iii. Practise words with ŋ and z, as in *sings*. (LEVEL C only)

PRACTICE 77

LEVEL C Practise saying:
swing swings sing sings bang bangs ring rings bring brings

iv. Practise words with 'ing' ending, like *reading*. Take care
not to stress the last syllable.

PRACTICE 78

LEVEL A Practise saying:
paint painting cut cutting draw drawing eat eating write
writing rain raining cross crossing run running jump
jumping skip skipping walk walking go going

LEVEL B Practise saying:
play playing bounce bouncing brush brushing catch catching
cry crying fight fighting eat eating hit hitting hurt hurting
kick kicking laugh laughing listen listening measure
measuring weigh weighing

LEVEL C Practise saying:
swing swinging sing singing bang banging think thinking
do doing go going read reading swim swimming wear
wearing come coming hang hanging try trying

v. Practise these in sentences.

PRACTICE 79

LEVEL A She's crossing the road.
She's crossing the road with the crossing man.
Tony's jumping.
Tony's jumping and Carol's skipping.
I'm going shopping.
Is it raining?
Thank you!
He's drawing a triangle.
He's painting a pink triangle.

LEVEL B   The donkey's hungry.
It's eating lots of carrots.
Longer than that one.
This monkey's tail is longer than that one.
He's measuring string.
How long is it?

LEVEL C   I rang you up.
I rang you up yesterday evening.
They're going to sing.
They're going to sing that song.
They're going to sing that song this evening.
I hope she brings her friend.
It makes a big bang.

18.1   h **as in** *hot*

Concerns: Italians

Problem: leaving h off the beginning of words, so that *hit* becomes *it*.

Ear training

DISTINGUISHING WORDS BEGINNING WITH h AND WORDS BEGINNING WITH A VOWEL.

PRACTICE 80

LEVEL A   Same/different practice:
hat at   who ooh   his is

LEVEL B   Same/different practice:
how ow   hall all   high eye   hill ill

LEVEL C   Same/different practice:
hair air   hold old   hitch itch   had add   hear ear

Production

i. Practise blowing out matches. Get the children simply to open their mouths and breathe out forcefully, rather than pursing their lips and blowing. This breathing sound should be just audible.

ii. Practise this sound at the beginning of words like *it* and *at*, to produce *hit* and *hat*. The h will then have to be made rather more gently and unobtrusively. Use the material in PRACTICE 80 above.

iii. Practise word pairs like *hit* and *it*. Use the material in PRACTICE 80 above.

iv. Practise more h words.

PRACTICE 81

LEVEL A   *hook hop her home house hair hand hot who how his whose hat here husband*

LEVEL B   *half heavy help hose harbour hide hen horse how high hill who head hurts happy*

LEVEL C   *whoever household hundred hold head hole hedge help hid husband hen hide horses house has*

v. Practise words with h in a mid-position. (LEVEL C only)

PRACTICE 82

LEVEL C   *behind ahead behave*

vi. Practise in sentences.

PRACTICE 83

LEVEL A   Who's eating my apple?
How much are the oranges?
Whose hat is this?
Here's her husband.

LEVEL B   How high is that hill?
Who feels ill?
How is his eye today?
My head hurts.
He's happy.

LEVEL C   Who is the head of the household?
My husband is holding his head because he has earache.
Harry Hardy's hen has got through a hole in the hedge.
Help me hide the horses behind the house.

18.2   **h as in *hot***

Concerns: Greek speakers

Problem: using the Scottish sound as in *loch* instead of h, or perhaps pronouncing it hj.

Ear training

English h must be taught as a new sound. Get the children to listen to you very carefully and then to experiment themselves while you listen unobtrusively.

Production

i. Practise words with h followed by 'back' vowels, like *horse* and *who*. (See page 15 for a chart showing which are 'back' vowels.)

PRACTICE 84

LEVEL A Practise saying:
hook   who   hop   house   hot   half   how   husband

LEVEL B Practise saying:
hungry   hose   harbour   horse   whose

LEVEL C Practise saying:
hunt   hall   hope   home   honey   hole   hoot   horrible   horn   horses   house

ii. Practise words with h followed by other vowels.

PRACTICE 85

LEVEL A Practise saying:
hat   he   hair   hand   head

LEVEL B Practise saying:
happy   heavy   headache   him   have   hill   he's   hens

LEVEL C Practise saying:
hen   habit   hail   heel   height   help   hip   health   haggle   hedge   hardly

iii. Practise in sentences.

PRACTICE 86

LEVEL A Who's hopping?
She's washing her hair.
Who's got a big hat?
His hat is in his hand.
This is her husband.

LEVEL B He's not very happy because he's got a headache.
How high is that hill?
Have you got any hens?
I saw him at the harbour.
Whose horse is that?

LEVEL C Harry Hardy's hen has got through a hole in the hedge.
Help me hide the horses behind the house.

What's the height of the highest hill?
He's hurt his heel.
He has the habit of haggling.
This horn hardly hoots at all.
I hope we have some honey at home.

---

19   l **as in** *lead*

Concerns: Indians, Pakistanis, Greek and Italian speakers

Problem: English has one l sound at the beginning of words
and before vowels (the 'clear' l) and another l sound (the
'dark' l) at the end of words or before consonants as in *hill* or
help. The difference between these two l sounds is not essential
for distinguishing different words, but with a class that is
progressing well, it is useful to teach the difference.

Ear training

Let the children listen to you carefully. The 'clear' l, as in *look*
and *below*, will come naturally to them, so make them pay
particular attention to your pronunciation of words like *hill*
and *help* where we use the 'dark' l. Use the material in
PRACTICE 87 and 88 below.

Production

i. Practise words with 'clear' l, where there should be no
difficulty at all.

PRACTICE 87

LEVEL A   Practise saying:
*lost   look   left   listen   lollipop   yellow   shilling   blue   black
plane   please*

LEVEL B   Practise saying:
*lino   lemon   light   collar   umbrella   eleven   cloud   plum
floor   climb   like   black   please*

LEVEL C   Practise saying:
*live   let   large   land   lose   loose   please   close   fly   allow
believe   lamb   family   flowers*

ii. Practise 'dark' l. A good approach to this is
'loolooloolloo . . . .', which 'finds' 'dark' l, the mouth being
drawn to the necessary position by the vowel uː. Compare this,
if necessary with 'leeleeleeleelee . . . .' which, by virtue of the

vowel sound, i:, produces 'clear' l. Now practise words with 'dark' l.

PRACTICE 88

LEVEL A   Practise saying:
small   milk   pencil   table   towel   ball   bottle   twelve
circle   triangle   sandals

LEVEL B   Practise saying:
stall   tell   full   scales   tall   daffodil   film   belt   apple
cupful   lable   girl   twelve   milk

LEVEL C   Practise saying:
all   fill   sell   tell   told   fold   filled   sold   detail   kettle
metal   health   steal   mail   fail   still

iii. Practise these in sentences.

PRACTICE 89

LEVEL A   Please look on the table.
Put some milk in the bottle.
I've got a small blue pencil.
I've found a towel.
Please listen.
Twelve yellow lollipops.

LEVEL B   A basket full of apples.
The tall girl with a black umbrella.
Tell Carol about the film.
Twelve cupfuls of milk.
I'd like some daffodils please.
There are lemons, plums and apples on the stall.

LEVEL C   He sells metal, I believe.
They told him all the details.
The Lamb family lives in London.
They sold all the flowers.
Please let me fill the kettle.

---

20   r **as in** *read*

Concerns: Indians, Pakistanis and Italian speakers

Problem: making 'English' r sounds. Two 'un-English' r sounds which should be avoided are the 'retroflex' one, used by many Indians and Pakistanis, where the tip of the tongue is bent back, producing a very distinctive sound which affects surrounding vowel sounds, and the Italian 'trilled' r.

Ear training

Start with r as a new sound, unrelated to any similar sound in the child's first language. Get the children to listen very carefully to your examples and then let them experiment while you listen to them. Use the material in PRACTICE 90 below.

Production

i. Practise words beginning with r, like *read.*

PRACTICE 90

LEVEL A Practise saying:
red run right rubber ruler rope roof rain rose reading room

LEVEL B Practise saying:
ran rocket raygun railway river rough road rabbit reptile rice

LEVEL C Practise saying:
red write rest rope rich really radio rain ripe rock ready

ii. Practise words with r in a cluster, like *tree.*

PRACTICE 91

LEVEL A Practise saying:
green three train drink drying grocer triangle grapes

LEVEL B Practise saying:
front dress frying-pan brother frightened grass programme broken crosses bridge

LEVEL C Practise saying:
grow cry friend throat bread breakfast crime crack prepare programme country umbrella train

iii. Practise words with r in mid-position.

PRACTICE 92

LEVEL A Practise saying:
orange different tomorrow January very

LEVEL B Practise saying:
squirrel measuring temperature earache paraffin dangerous very

98

LEVEL C   Practise saying:

serious   *sorry*   *carry*   *career*   *parents*   *salary*   *factory*   *hurry*

iv. Practise in sentences.

PRACTICE 93

LEVEL A   x   Carol! What are you reading?
            y   I'm reading 'The red train to Bradford'.
            x   Can I read it tomorrow please?
            y   Yes. It's a very good book.

LEVEL B   The spacemen ran to their rocket.
            The rabbit was very frightened.
            The railway crosses a dangerous bridge.
            Squirrels aren't reptiles.
            This road is very rough.
            She's measuring rice into a frying-pan.

LEVEL C   She turned on the radio and got breakfast ready.
            There was a serious programme about crime in the country.
            It was raining, so she took her red umbrella.
            On the train she read a letter from her parents and one from a friend.
            The factory pays him a very high salary.

21.1   Words that end with voiced consonants

Concerns: Greek, and also Italian and Turkish speakers, but see **21.2** below.

Problem: words that end with voiced consonants: b, d, g, v, z, ð as in *with*, and dʒ as in *edge*. Greek speakers will substitute voiceless consonants, making *had* into *hat*, etc. The problem is greatest when such words come at the end of the sentence. Exceptions for Greek speakers are l and n which they can manage in final position. Italian and Turkish speakers will tend to add an additional vowel sound.

Ear training

DISTINGUISHING VOICED AND VOICELESS CONSONANTS AT THE END OF WORDS.

PRACTICE 94

LEVEL A   Pick out the words with final b:
            kerb   *hop*   *shop*   *cup*   *up*

Pick out the words with final d:

did hat *date* what *cloud* nut wet *red* hot

Pick out the words with final g:

big fork *bag* back peg *plug* black *egg* hook *leg*
flag

LEVEL B Same/different practice:

hat had   write ride   feet feed   leaf leave

Pick out the words with final b:

web wrap keep top cheap

Pick out the words with final d:

made kite *bird* slide *light* sad *tired* feet throat
shout *wood* set *shed*

Pick out the words with final g:

dog walk dark *frog* kick *dig* lake talk *egg* bark

LEVEL C Same/different practice:

coat code   white wide   bought board   built build   beat bead
relief relieve   belief believe   leaf leave   rip rib   rope robe
hiss his   Dick dig   duck dug   docks dogs   safe save   half halve

Production

i. Practise words like *reading*, of which the first syllable ends
in a voiced consonant but where there is also a suffix. There
should be no difficulty in saying these.

PRACTICE 95

LEVEL A Practise saying:

reading standing *windy* cloudy *foggy*

LEVEL B Practise saying:

feeding riding *leaving* digging *bigger* giving *bending*
folding changing

LEVEL C Practise saying:

builder saving *wider* ladder *Peggy* nobbly *rubbing*
snobbish dragging *jogging* living

ii. Split the words in the last practice into two parts, e.g. *read*
and its ending, *ing*, and practise in this way. Then forget about
the second parts and practise the first parts as words in their
own right. Alternatively, ask the child to say each word slowly
and halt him just as he is about to say the second syllable.
It is particularly important that these final voiced consonant
sounds should be audible at the end of sentences.

iii. Practise more words ending with voiced consonants.

PRACTICE 96

LEVEL A   Practise saying:
*with   live   have   nose   head   shoes   bed   please   red   bag
flag   leg   kerb*

LEVEL B   Practise saying:
*suede   move   lose   need   card   cheese   food   bird   web
big   dog   frog   stream   bag   egg   cupboard*

LEVEL C   Practise saying:
*nib   job   cave   weave   judge   page   arrive   rose   sees
road   bag   college   dog   dug   good   robe   red   gold
said   believe*

iv. Practise in sentences, paying particular attention to voiced
consonants when they come at the end of words at the end of
sentences.

PRACTICE 97

LEVEL A   Can I have a red bag please?
The green flag is mine.
I've broken my leg.
Stop at the kerb.
These black clouds are very big.

LEVEL B   Don't feed these birds.
The spider makes a big web.
The dog chased the frog into the stream.
This bag is made of brown suede.
Move these eggs please, and put them in the cupboard.

LEVEL C   I live in Kings Road, Leeds.
The dog dug a big hole in the ground.
He's got a very good job at the college.
The Queen wore robes of gold, black and red.
Bob said that nothing was wrong, but did you believe him?

21.2   Words ending with any consonants

Concerns: Italians, Turkish speakers, and some Indians and
Pakistanis

Problem: overcoming the tendency to add an extra vowel
sound.

Ear training

DISTINGUISHING WORD PAIRS LIKE *jump jumping   ride rider.*
(LEVELS B and C only).

PRACTICE 98

LEVEL B   Same/different practice:
sad sadder   big bigger   cheap cheaper   tall taller   safe safer
clean cleaner   old older   farm farmer   cook cooker
but butter   let letter

LEVEL C   Same/different practice:
rub rubber   lad ladder   late later   lard larder   paint painter
teach teacher   write writer   play player   work worker
nice nicer   rough rougher   hard harder

Production

i. Practise words with a vowel ending like *writer*, which
should be straightforward.

PRACTICE 99

LEVEL A   Practise saying:
paper   zebra   dinner   grocer   collar   sweater   pullover
leather   shoulder   finger   cooker

LEVEL B   Practise saying:
sadder   bigger   cheaper   taller   safer   cleaner   older   farmer
butter   letter   cooker   doctor   brother   mother   sister
father

LEVEL C   Practise saying:
rubber   ladder   later   larder   painter   teacher   writer
player   worker   nicer   rougher   harder   richer   quicker
bigger   smaller

ii. Practise the words like *sadder* – the second word in each pair
of PRACTICE 98 above – in two halves: *sadd – er*. The second half
can then be dropped, to leave the word with a consonant
ending, like *sad*. The alternative method is to get the child to
say *sadder* slowly and deliberately, then to repeat it; on the
second occasion you stop him just as he reaches the d sound.
Use the material in PRACTICE 99 above. (LEVELS B and C only).
With children at LEVEL A use the second method described
above; when they try to add an extra vowel sound to words
like *hop*, producing something like 'hopper', halt them just
as they get to the p sound. For this, use material in PRACTICE
100 below.

102

LEVEL A   Practise saying:

skip cheap rope zip kerb coat hat cloud book
fog bag home safe roof five bus with sun pen
green old room oblong ball wool cars trees days
flowers shoes his Tony's Carol's buses house houses
pieces ounces pens books balls ropes hats coats bags
dogs clouds eggs shillings pounds months

LEVEL B   Practise saying:

cheap web kite night slide bird hide pick park
peck with bad squeak frog dog grass bees beads
bridge gun stream sting wrong swing birds leaves
slides swings guns beaches streams animals frogs
worms digs hides pecks squeaks stings builds catches
chased first chewed

LEVEL C   Practise saying:

time got ticket take side tired wife both bag laugh
give please case miss must run ways rush much
long carriage large train return fill come hang
times tickets minutes sides backs bags laughs gives
cases rushes catches edges carriages fills comes hangs

iii. Practise in sentences.

LEVEL A   X Where's Carol's pen?
         Y Carol's pen! Where's *your* pen?
         X I've lost it.
         Y Carol's got her pen in her bag; and she's at home.

Can I have six ounces of wool please?
Is this Carol's skipping rope?
I can't draw an oblong.
Yes, you can!
These cars are very cheap.
Are these trees safe? They're very old.

LEVEL B   X What's Uncle Jim doing in the park?
         Y He's flying Tony's kite.
         X Where are Tony and Carol?
         Y They're with Uncle Jim.
         X Hallo Uncle Jim! What's wrong?
         Z The dog has broken the kite.
         X Oh dear. How?

z First he chased it. Then he chewed it.

x Oh, bad dog!

x Hurry up! We must rush. Or we'll miss the train!

y Oh I can't run any farther. I'm too tired!

x Oh please try!

y How much time have we got?

x Three minutes. Do come on! Look – I'll take this large bag.

y Oof! Thank you. That's better. I'll run ahead and get the tickets.

x Here we are. Phew! We've done it!

y Look! Here is Bob, and his wife is with him.

x Oh – what a long time since I last saw them.

y Hallo – how are you both?

22.1 Consonant clusters

Concerns: Indians and Pakistanis

Problem: clusters at the beginning of words, especially where the second consonant is *other* than r, l, w or j. The words that will be the greatest problem will therefore be *stop*, *sky*, *spot*, etc, – most of those beginning with s. These children will either slip in an initial vowel sound, so that *stop* becomes 'istop', or they will put a vowel sound into the cluster, producing 'sitop'.

Ear training

Rhythm practice is important here, because rhythm is connected with the number of syllables in a word, and the child who inserts extra vowels is creating extra syllables and so distorting the overall rhythm. Practise these words in groups, and beat the rhythms. Be on the watch out for extra syllable-beat at the points where the clusters come. Alternatively, draw the various rhythm patterns on the blackboard, number them, and get the children to match each word you say to the right pattern. Thus *school* is a one-syllable word and can be represented by one large square:□ *skipping rope* has three syllables and can be represented by one large square, one small and another large one:□ ▫ □

PRACTICE 102

school   skipping rope
smooth   snow   scarf
King street

scales   spoon   stove
stand up
stop at the kerb

LEVEL B   *squirrel   snake   spider*
star   spaceman   screen
stethoscope   scales
stone   smallest
stamp   stationery   string
spring   stream
smoke
stripe   striped   skin

LEVEL C   *skill   score   scratch*
straight   stop
stupid
small   sneeze
stretch   square   slow
snack

Production

i. Take the words in the last practice one by one. First let the children beat or identify the rhythms, and then let them repeat after you, while you beat the rhythm silently to them. If an extra vowel creeps in at this stage, make the children omit the first consonant of the cluster, practising 'top' instead of *stop*, for example. Repeat 'top' three times to a steady beat. Then without altering the beat, try *stop* three times. Experiment a little to find the best speed. These clusters tend to persist as problems, so be content with slight but steady improvement. The most important thing is to get the rhythm right. Do exaggerate the stress of the stressed syllables and weaken the unstressed ones. Use the material in PRACTICE 102 above,

ii. Practise in sentences, beating rhythms first.

PRACTICE 103

LEVEL A   This is King Street School.
The snow is very smooth.
She's wearing a red scarf.
Stand up and don't talk!
The scales are under the stall.
Who's spilt the milk?

LEVEL B   That squirrel has stripes!
The doctor put on his stethoscope.

He went behind the screen.
The snake has lost its old skin.
The small boy has stomach ache.

LEVEL C Sloane Square is straight ahead.
The match was scratched, so no one scored.
It would be stupid to stop now.
I had a small snack.

22.2 Consonant clusters

Concerns: Indians and Pakistanis

Problem: clusters at the end of words. The children may want
to put a vowel into the cluster, making *milk* into 'miluk'; they
may reverse the elements of some clusters, making *desk* into
'deks'; they may not pronounce all the elements.

Ear training

Rhythm is important here. See the notes on this under
Problem **22.1** above; the same techniques apply here, but
use the material printed below.

PRACTICE 104

LEVEL A *desk   desks   shelf*
milk
belt   belts   vest   vests
cat   cats
old   soft
jump
finished
spilt   lost

LEVEL B *washed   film*
jumped   skipped   walked
jumped   went
spoons   forks
looked   listened   changed
brushed   combed

LEVEL C *kept   cups*
collapsed
robs   robbed
rats
eighth   eights

width   widths
locks   locked
lamp   won't
hints   pens
end   ends
ninth   ninths
minced   lunch   fridge
length   lengths
help
helps   helped   hold   holds
milk   shelf
film   films   filmed
health   else
pills   old   felt
laughed   fifth   fifths
bulge
rifts   halves   halved
wasp   wasps
haste   hosts   ask
asks   pleased   wished   watched
lodge   lodged

Production

i. Practise saying words with final clusters in short phrases
or sentences, so that a word beginning with a vowel
follows each word with a final cluster, as in *the desk in
the corner*. Beat the rhythms out first. Ignore, for the time
being, any other difficulties that arise, but omit any sentence
that presents too many other difficulties for your particular
children. Make sure the vocabulary and structural patterns
involved are already familiar. The child who reverses the
sounds in a cluster, saying, for example, 'deks', needs to have
this pointed out and to have an opportunity to experiment
with the right order; he will probably continue to say it wrong
from time to time and you will have to remind him gently.
The more serious problem is the intervening vowel, because
it throws out the speech rhythm. To focus attention on the
rhythm, apply the techniques described in **22.1** above. Where
one of the component sounds can be prolonged, as for
example with s, lengthen it a little.

PRACTICE 105

LEVEL A   This desk is mine.

The milk is on the table.
The milk's on the table.
A soft apple.
Can I have a soft apple please?
Jump on your chair.
The cat's under the table.

LEVEL B   Put the spoons and forks on the table.
She washed a jersey.
He jumped into the car.
She skipped along the road.
He walked out of the house.
They looked at television.

LEVEL C   He kept a lot of cups in the cupboard.
The man collapsed and died.
The thief robbed a rich woman.
The kids are in the garden.
We helped a policeman.
He won't answer my question.
What's the bulge in that bag?
Ask Alan, or else ask Eddy.
Three-fifths and a half.

ii. Practise sentences with several clusters, some of them at the end of the sentence. Some of the clusters come before words beginning with consonants, which in effect, enlarges the cluster.

PRACTICE 106

LEVEL A   Stand on your desks.
I've finished my milk.
Look right, look left.
The dog's eating my belt!
I've hurt my hand.
One, two, three – jump!
He's lost his vest.

LEVEL B   She washed her hair.
She washed, brushed and combed it.
We watched a film on television.
The doctor wrote a prescription.
The spacemen wore big helmets.
They climbed the mountains.
She skipped, jumped and hopped.

Please put the milk in the fridge.
They thumbed a lift to London.
He's the eighth person to collapse.
Its width is three and three-eighths inches.
We've got mince and carrots for lunch.
They won't give any helpful hints.
He went to great lengths to solve the problem.
The length is four and four-fifths.
I had lodgings in Leeds.
They laughed, themselves.

22.3 Consonant clusters

Concerns: Greek Cypriots

Problem: all-voiced final clusters will be made voiceless, so
that *dogs* will become *docks*. Final clusters which are mixed
voiced and voiceless will also be difficult, but see **22.6** below
for this. Final clusters containing n will also be hard, and
words like *ant/and/add* confused.

Ear training
i. DISTINGUISHING PAIRS LIKE *dogs/docks*. (LEVELS B and C only)

PRACTICE 107

LEVEL B   Same/different practice:
pegs pecks   bags backs   eggs X (name of the letter)   *cards carts*

LEVEL C   Same/different practice:
rides writes   dogs docks   ribs rips   logs locks

ii. DISTINGUISHING WORDS LIKE *ant/and/add*. (LEVELS B and C
only)

PRACTICE 108

LEVEL B   Same/different practice:
ant and   sent send   said send   sent said

LEVEL C   Same/different practice:
*land lad   lend led   lent lend   led lend   lent led   and add
ant add   and ant*

Production
i. Practise final voiced clusters as in do*gs*. The difficulty lies

first in distinguishing these from their voiceless counterparts, and secondly, in their final position. Overcome the final position difficulty by practising these words before words beginning with vowels, using PRACTICE 105 above. In the exercise below, each cluster appears first before a word with a vowel, and then on its own.

PRACTICE 109

LEVEL A Practise saying:

The flags are green.   These spoons are old.
Flags   Spoons
The roads are wet.   The wind is warm.
Roads   Wind
These combs are plastic.   This orange is cheap.
Combs   Orange
Her hand is wet.   The plums are green.
Hand   Plums
The dogs are small.   The stalls are big.
Dogs   Stalls
                              My gloves are black.
                              Gloves

LEVEL B He comes at five.   The frogs are jumping.
Comes   Frogs
She phones every day.   Pigeons are grey.
Phones   Pigeons
Those hills are high.   Their scales are dry.
Hills   Scales
This island is big.   Lions are fierce.
Island   Lions
The land is dry.   Lambs are gentle.
Land   Lambs
The lines are black.   The crocodiles are hungry.
Lines   Crocodiles
The streams are full.   These bags are yellow.
Streams   Bags
The tunnels are long.   The eggs are brown.
Tunnels   Eggs
It feeds on grass.   Those cards are Tony's.
Feeds   Cards

LEVEL C Her bags are heavy.   She rides a bicycle.
Bags   Rides

110

Our pens are broken.   The dogs are barking.
Pens   Dogs
The end of the road.   All the logs are dry.
End   Logs
The ends of the ribbon.
Ends

ii. Practise words like *ant/and/add* separately. (LEVELS B and C only)

PRACTICE 110

LEVEL B   Practise saying:
ant   and   sent   send   said

LEVEL C   Practise saying:
ant   and   add   land   lad   lend   lent   led

iii. Practise all these problems in sentences.

PRACTICE 111

LEVEL B   X Send a letter to Tony.
           Y I sent one yesterday. I wrote it at the weekend.
           X Tell me what you said.
           Y I wrote about school and about my dogs.

LEVEL C   X Hallo Eddy. This is my friend Fred.
           Y Hallo!
           Z Hallo!
           Y Could you please lend me two shillings.
           X Yes – Oh dear. Sorry! I've only got sixpence.
           Z I've got two shillings. Here you are.
           Y Thank you. I'll let you have it back tomorrow.
           Z I must go now.
           X Oh – why?
           Z I've got to get some logs for my mother. And some coal.
           X That sounds a lot. Can I give you a hand?
           Y Let me help too.
           Z Thank you both very much. That'll be wonderful.

22.4   **Consonant clusters**

Concerns: Indians, Pakistanis and Italians

Problem: With clusters across word boundaries, as in *his coat*, *what's she* doing? etc.

Ear training

First, establish the rhythm, letting the children beat out each word group or identifying the rhythm visually using big squares and small squares (see PRACTICE 102 above).

PRACTICE 112

LEVEL A

On the table.   Where's she going?   Rough paper.
In Tony's hand.   Some peaches.   Warm coat.
Tony's pocket.   Some nuts.   I've finished.
With Tony.   On Saturday.   I've got one.
Ten past eight.   On Thursday.   Five to six.
A big red apple.   How much change?   Ten to nine.

LEVEL B

Some milk.   We played football.   Ten years ago.
Some chalk.   Inside the cinema.   Nineteen sixty-nine.
He's painted it.   Outside the house.   These buses.
He's made a book.   Then she laughed.   I'm not hungry.
Thirteen times.   When did you come?   Give Tony a book.
Five times.   Five years ago.

LEVEL C

It has been done.   I'll finish it.
At the weekend.   He'll go.
Let him come.   I like cycling.
All the morning.   Please move your feet.
I did thank him.   Which day?
That's a bad thing.   Which room?
There's your phone call.   Please type this.
Finish that job.

Production

i. Take the phrases in the last practice one at a time. Let the children beat out each one first, and then repeat each one after you, carefully and deliberately, but bringing out the rhythm. Be particularly strict in not allowing vowel sounds to slip into the clusters, whether within or between words. Also discourage gaps between words. Aim at a smooth succession of component sounds in each cluster.

ii. Tackle clusters with more than two component sounds. First work on the words individually, identifying rhythm patterns to help avoid extra syllables; then take the groups together. If something has to be sacrificed, let it be an occasional consonant, but never the rhythm. It is better however if all the component sounds are audible in smooth succession. An example of feasible consonant-dropping arises in *What's she doing?* where the central s sound might well be omitted in order to preserve the overall rhythm. It can be difficult even for native speakers to sound every component consonant in such clusters.

PRACTICE 113

LEVEL A

What's this?
It's mine.
It's green.
It's blue.
It's brown.
It's Tony's.
It's Carol's.
An orange book.
An orange dress.
A small brown egg.
What's the time?
What's she doing?

Quarter past six.
It's quarter past six.
It's quarter past five.
I went shopping.
Amarjit's coat.
Carol's book.
Uncle Jim's shop.
Smooth skin.
I've broken it.
He isn't reading it.
She isn't cooking.
He isn't washing the car.

LEVEL B

Some plasticine.
Six times.
Last week.
Last year.
Last Monday.

About spacemen.
The smallest child.
The dearest fruit.
I like space films.
First she stood up.

LEVEL C

It isn't snowing.
We aren't going.
I'm trying to help.
Which train?
I've fried some fish.
Quarter past three.
It's quarter past three.
He'll drive.
It's cracked.
Six students.
The last programme.

The best reason.
The thirteenth chapter.
What's she called?
That's most stupid.
He won three prizes.
Which is the correct form?
I've lost the spanner.
You don't need one.
Where's my clothes brush?
He's stopped smoking.

(Also – see Problem **23** below for more material.)

22.5 Consonant clusters

Concerns: all

Problem: clusters of more than two consonants, within a word, as in **street** or in two-part words like sta**mp-m**achine. This is mainly a question of preserving rhythm, once the constituent sounds have been mastered. Aim at making each consonant audible.

Ear training

RHYTHM WORK

Get the children beating out the rhythms of word sets. Watch out for extra beats indicating a tendency to make extra syllables. Use the material in PRACTICES 114, 115, 116 and 117 below.

Production

i. Practise words with initial clusters, beating or identifying the rhythms first. (See PRACTICE 102 above)

PRACTICE 114

LEVEL A   Practise saying:
street   square

LEVEL B   Practise saying:
squirrel   striped   stream

LEVEL C   Practise saying:

strong   scream   streak   squeak   strange   strike

ii. Practise mid-word clusters, building them up bit by bit, always preserving the word rhythm.

PRACTICE 115

LEVEL A   Practise saying:
children   Wednesday   greengrocer   umbrella   grandmother grandfather

LEVEL B   Practise saying:
hungry   prescription   country   stamp-machine   postcard postman   England   children

LEVEL C   Practise saying:
appointment   factory   electricity   exchange   experience employer   complicated   transport   display   export

iii. Practise final clusters in the same way. (LEVELS B and C only)

PRACTICE 116

LEVEL B Practise saying:
jumped   helped   collects   posts   fields   drinks
doesn't   chemist's

LEVEL C Practise saying:
thanked   sixth   holds   films   students   appointments
products

iv. Practise sentences with these and inter-word clusters.

PRACTICE 117

LEVEL A x Is this King Street?
Y Yes, it is.
x Where's the greengrocer's please?
Y It's here, in front of you.
x Oh yes. Thank you.
x I've lost my umbrella.
Y Oh dear. Where?
x At the greengrocer's.
Y When?
x On Wednesday afternoon.

LEVEL B The squirrel jumped from tree to tree.
The doctor wrote a prescription.
The postman filled the stamp-machine.
The children were very hungry.

LEVEL C He thanked his employer.
I have an appointment at the factory.
This is the sixth electricity cut in five days.
My work is complicated.
Can you please arrange transport?
There will be a display of products during the conference.

22.6   Consonant clusters

Concerns: Greek Cypriots and Italians

Problems: where voiced and voiceless consonants are involved
in the same cluster, as in *tree* or *blackboard*. (See page 18
for lists of voiced and voiceless consonants.) *Blackboard*
may become 'blagboard', both consonants getting voiced; and

115

in *tree*, the r sound may affect the t, so that it gets voiced too, the whole word emerging as 'dree'. There will be the greatest confusion where such clusters occur at the end of words, particularly where they are also at the end of a sentence. Words with 'x' in them, and pronounced gz, will confuse the children also, since this letter is usually pronounced ks in Greek; so they will tend to pronounce *example* and *exam* as 'eksample' and 'eksam'. Italians will find initial sl, sm and sn hard, replacing them with zl, zm and zn respectively.

Ear training

DISTINGUISHING PAIRS LIKE ***try/dry***. (LEVEL C only).

PRACTICE 118

LEVEL C   Same/different practice:
try dry   class glass   train drain   true drew   plot blot

Production

i. Practise clusters with p, t or k in second position in a cluster, as in *jumping*, *painting*, or *thinking*. (LEVELS B and C only)

PRACTICE 119

LEVEL B   Practise saying:
seventeen painted mountain sometimes timetable winter

LEVEL C   Practise saying:
important intend complaint alcohol income dentist entertainment intelligent wanted import

ii. Practise these in sentences where there are also clusters with all voiced consonants. (LEVELS B and C only)

PRACTICE 120

LEVEL B   He's painted a picture.
She's sixteen or seventeen.
The timetable says there are three afternoon trains to Bradford.
They climbed the mountain.

LEVEL C   This complaint is important.
I wanted an appointment with the dentist.
What is the annual income?

116

Does he drink alcohol?
There's to be some entertainment on the last evening of the conference. (N.B. See also Problem **23** below.)

iii. Now practise other mixed clusters, like *try*.

PRACTICE 121

LEVEL A   Practise saying:
flag   three   friend   from   plane   please   crossing   policeman
trousers   plastic   sweeping   washbasin   pencil   class   clock
crayon   cloakroom   bathroom
For Italians especially: *sleeping   small   snowing*

LEVEL B   Practise saying:
front   frightened   plough   cream
For Italians especially: *smaller   smoke   snake   slide   slow*

LEVEL C   Practise saying:
throat   throw   frost   plan   trust   treatment   crowd   crack
switch   answer   dance
For Italians especially: *slot   slip   smile   snack   sneeze*
(See also Problem **23** below.)

iv. Practise in sentences, looking out also for clusters between words.

PRACTICE 122

LEVEL A   The washbasin is in the bathroom.
The policeman is wearing a blue plastic jacket.
My friend is from Cyprus.
Have you got any pink paint?
The small dog is sleeping.

LEVEL B   I've painted that mountain in winter.
Please buy me some cream for lunch.
They're sliding on the ice.
Those children are throwing snowballs.

LEVEL C   Your sore throat needs treatment.
When you turn on this switch, the electricity crackles.
The entrance to their flat is at the front of the building.
There was a large crowd at the dance.
A smiling man came into the snackbar.

23 Incomplete plosion

23.1 Clusters with two plosives like *blackboard*

Concerns: all

Problem: mid- or inter-word clusters, where there are two plosive consonants, (i.e. two of the following: p, b, t, d, k, g). In such clusters the first of the two consonants is not pronounced fully. The mouth assumes the correct position for the first one, but the breath that would normally be released explosively with it is retained and released with the following consonant. The fault you will hear is complete separation of the two consonants, or even an inserted vowel, producing 'blackaboard' and 'a hot-a-day'.

Ear training

RHYTHM WORK

Have the children beat out the rhythms of the following material, and let them listen critically to each other.

PRACTICE 123

LEVEL A

Blackboard.
Sit down.
A black book.
A red pen.
It's market day.
A silk tie.
Here's a white bus.
A pink dress.
I saw eight boys.

This is my suitcase.
Dark green.
A plastic bag.
A big bag.
It's a hot day.
His wet coat.
That peach.
Or light blue.

LEVEL B

Eight times.
The third time.
A cheap day return.
An old cat.
My favourite programme.
I want to play.

The biggest book.
The cheapest tickets.
White paper.
It's an old dog.
He didn't go.
He can't cook.

118

LEVEL C Half past ten.   A cheque book.
Night time.   An old problem.
A good programme.   What did he say?
A bad day.   The youngest boy.
Did Tony go?   Good-bye.

Production

i. Practise the part of the phrase that contains the cluster in isolation, and then the phrase as a whole. Use the material in the last practice.

ii. Practise these sentences in the same way, paying great attention to rhythm.

PRACTICE 124

LEVEL A Write it on the blackboard.
Sit down and open your red books.
Where's the red pen?
Can I have the black book?
It's market day in Bradford.
We bought a silk tie.
It's dark green.

LEVEL B How can I get to the park?
She can't cook cabbage.
The next train is at half past two.
The old dog sat under the tree.
What's your favourite programme?
They walked to the station.
He jumped ten feet.

LEVEL C I had a bad day at work.
I lost two files.
The youngest typist gave in her notice.
What did she say?
She said she had to work too hard.
That's an old problem.
She cooked the meal.
He slipped on the ice.
They thanked him.
He robbed a bank.
The shelf sagged a little.

119

23.2   Nasal plosion

Concerns: all

Problem: with mid-word clusters or clusters between words, where there is a plosive consonant (i.e., p, b, t, d, k or g) followed by a nasal consonant, (n, m or ŋ as in si**ng**); the breath normally released with the plosive consonant is let out nasally with the nasal consonant. Look out for mispronunciations like 'postaman'.

Ear training

RHYTHM BEATING, AS FOR TWO-PLOSIVE CLUSTERS (described in **23.1** above).

PRACTICE 125

LEVEL A
Good **m**orning.
Is it **m**ine?
We saw an ol**d m**an.
I've spilt **m**y milk.

I've finishe**d m**y book.
This is my gran**dm**other.
I bought a re**d m**at.
This is a goo**d n**ewspaper.

LEVEL B
Chris**tm**as time.
There's the pos**tm**an.
What's the pos**tm**ark?

Here's our compar**tm**ent.
It's a white **m**ouse.
Where's the stamp-**m**achine?

LEVEL C
Have you a halfpenny? (- Hap'ny)
My right **kn**ee hurts.
There is the night **n**urse.
Ask the depar**tm**ent **m**anager.

Let's have a hot **m**eal.
What a loud **n**oise.
He's an ol**d m**an.

Production

i. Practise saying the material in the last practice.

ii. Practise this additional material, beating the rhythm of each sentence before saying it.

PRACTICE 126

LEVEL A
Goo**d m**orning Mr. Brown.
I've lost **m**y hat.
This is my gran**dm**other's umbrella.

120

Where's the old mat?
Read newspapers and books.

LEVEL B I like melons.
They like nuts.

LEVEL C Two and sixpence halfpenny (-hap'ny)
Where is Fred Knight?
This is an old knife.
What a loud noise!

23.3 Lateral plosion

Concerns: all

Problem: with clusters mid-word or between words, where there is a plosive consonant (i.e., p, b, t, d, k or g) followed by l; the breath for the plosive consonant is retained and released with the l. Look out for mispronunciations like 'kalock' for *clock*.

Ear training

Beat the rhythms of the following groups of words.

PRACTICE 127

LEVEL A *class   clock*
cloakroom   plimsoll
black   plane
policeman
glove

LEVEL B *plough*
please   climb
plasticine
bleat   play   cliff   clean

LEVEL C *problem*
flat   blow   blame
blister   complain
plan   clue   clear   glass

E

Production

i. Practise saying the words in the last practice.

ii. Practise the following sentences, beating them first.

PRACTICE 128

LEVEL A   This is **cl**ass Three A.
Look at the **cl**ock.
My **pl**imsolls are in the **cl**oakroom.
I'm drawing a **bl**ack **pl**ane.
The **pol**iceman is wearing white **gl**oves.
Can I have some **bl**ack laces **pl**ease.

LEVEL B   The farmer **pl**oughs the fields.
They're **pl**aying with **pl**asticine.
He **cl**imbed the **cl**iff.
The goats are **bl**eating.
Please **cl**ean the **bl**ackboard.

LEVEL C   What is your problem?
I'm not com**pl**aining.
Nobody is to **bl**ame.
This is my **pl**an.
We need some **cl**ear **gl**ass.

Vowels

---

24   i **and** e **as in** *bit* **and** *bet*

Concerns: Indians and Pakistanis

Problem: making these two vowels sufficiently distinct from each
other.

Ear training

DISTINGUISHING WORD PAIRS OR IDENTIFYING e WORDS FROM LISTS.

PRACTICE 129

LEVEL A   Pick out the e words:
pen   desk   sit   red   men   big   wind   wet   egg   in   this

LEVEL B   Same/different practice:
tin ten   pick peck

Pick out the e words:
next   thick   letter   hen   chick   dig   web   shell   skin   peck
yes   get   dish   stick   hill   set

122

Same/different practice:
bit bet   wit wet   built belt   pin pen   disc desk   litter letter

Production

i. Practise i words.

PRACTICE 130

LEVEL A Practise saying:
sit   big   wind   in   this   his   milk   skip   dinner   zip   inch

LEVEL B Practise saying:
tin   thick   chick   dig   skin   dish   stick   hill   with   which   pick   hit   hitting   kick   kicking   squirrel   kitten   written   minute   six   sixty   him

LEVEL C Practise saying:
bit   pin   disc   wit   built   litter   fit   rid   thin   grin   will   fill   mill   print   hint   ill   till   if   live   ship   bin   written   milk

ii. Practise e words. The front of the tongue is slightly lower in the mouth here than for the vowel i. Both are short vowels.

PRACTICE 131

LEVEL A Practise saying:
pen   desk   red   men   wet   egg   ten   seven   bed   neck   leg   dress

LEVEL B Practise saying:
next   ten   peck   letter   hen   web   shell   yes   get   set   shed   lemon   then   help   very

LEVEL C Practise saying:
bet   pen   desk   wet   belt   letter   send   get   cheque   let   bread   said   mess   less

iii. Practise word pairs like *bit/bet* (LEVELS B and C only), or word lists involving both vowels (LEVEL A). Use the material in PRACTICE 129 above.

iv. Practise in sentences.

PRACTICE 132

LEVEL A This is a big desk.
Where's the red pen?
Can I have a ten-inch zip?
I bought some eggs and a pint of milk.

It's six minutes to ten.
Which letter comes from India?
The chick is pecking the eggshell.
This lemon has a very thick skin.

LEVEL C He put my letter in the litter-bin.
I've written you a cheque.
She said 'Buy some bread and milk'.
Let's get rid of this mess on the desk.

---

25 e and æ as in *bet* and *bat*

Concerns: all

Problem: making these two vowels sufficiently distinct from
each other.

Ear training

DISTINGUISHING WORD PAIRS OR IDENTIFYING æ WORDS IN LISTS.

PRACTICE 133

LEVEL A Same/different practice:
man men

Pick out the æ words:
*hat   tap   desk   pen   red   flag   man   left   bag   ten   seven
cat*

LEVEL B Same/different practice:
had head   sad said   pan pen

LEVEL C Same/different practice:
bad bed   lad led   land lend   bat bet

Production

i. Practise words with æ. The front of the tongue should be lower
in the mouth than for e, and the jaws slightly wider apart.

PRACTICE 134

LEVEL A Practise saying:
hat   tap   flag   man   bag   cat   apple   thank you   mac

LEVEL B Practise saying:
*had   sad   pan   than   land   ran   stamp   van   happy   angry
thank*

124

LEVEL C Practise saying:
bad bat lad land hand mat pack mad matter
manager packed

ii. Practise words with e. Use the material in PRACTICE 131 above.

iii. Practise pairs and lists involving both sounds. æ as in *bat* can be made fractionally longer than e if they otherwise sound too alike. Use the material in PRACTICE 133 above.

iv. Practise in sentences.

PRACTICE 135

LEVEL A This is a red hat.
My hat is red.
Can I have an apple?
Is this a cat or a man?
Here are ten flags.
Thank you.

LEVEL B She said thank you.
Put a stamp on the letter.
He's a very sad man.
He ran to the red van.

LEVEL C Have you packed the egg?
Who's batting next?
Fred's a bad lad.
I must mend the mat.
Can you lend me a hand?

---

26 ɑ:, æ **and** ʌ **as in** *cart*, *cat* **and** *cut*

Concerns: all

Problem: making these sufficiently distinct from each other.

Ear training

i. DISTINGUISHING ɑ: AND æ IN LISTS AND WORD PAIRS LIKE *cart/cat*.

PRACTICE 136

LEVEL A Pick out the ɑ: words:
car hat tap are cat scarf dark man aunt yard

LEVEL B Same/different practice:
cart cat   aunt ant

125

LEVEL C   Same/different practice:
heart hat   part pat   barn ban   park pack   mark mac

ii. DISTINGUISHING ɑː AND ʌ IN LISTS AND WORD PAIRS LIKE *cart/cut*.

PRACTICE 137

LEVEL A   Pick out the ɑː words:
aunt *plug one* **car** *bus up jump* **dark**

LEVEL B   Same/different practice:
cart cut   dark duck   March much

LEVEL C   Same/different practice:
*heart hut   staff stuff   barn bun   calf cuff   starter stutter
calm come*

iii. DISTINGUISHING ʌ AND æ IN LISTS AND WORD PAIRS LIKE *cut/cat*.

PRACTICE 138

LEVEL A   Pick out the ʌ words:
plug flag mat **one** *man bus* **up** *jump*

LEVEL B   Same/different practice:
cat cut   ran run

LEVEL C   Same/different practice:
cap cup   stamp stump   mad mud

Production

i. Practise words like *cart*, with the long vowel ɑː. Some
learners will pronounce an r sound after this vowel, particularly
if they have been exposed to English spelling. This matters
very little.

PRACTICE 139

LEVEL A   Practise saying:
aunt car dark bar after banana half halves are bath

LEVEL B   Practise saying:
cart dark star March castle harbour basket star

LEVEL C   Practise saying:
*heart starter laugh staff card part barn calf farmer
alarm*

ii. Practise words with æ like *bat*. Use the material in PRACTICE 134
above.

iii. Practise words with ʌ like *but*.

126

LEVEL A   Practise saying:
plug   one   bus   up   jump   rubber   number   button   cup

LEVEL B   Practise saying:
*cut   duck   much   run   sun   tongue   stomach   brushed   jump
once   come   Monday*

LEVEL C   Practise saying:
*hut   stuff   bun   cuff   stutter   cut   stump   much   mud   ton
judge   lunch*

iv. Practise these three vowel sounds in pairs and lists. Use the material in PRACTICES 136, 137 and 138 above.

v. Practise in sentences. Devote your attention to stressed syllables.

PRACTICE 141

LEVEL A   Can I have a banana?
Is it a bus or a car?
Half a bar of chocolate please.
My aunt's in the car.
The cat is dark brown or black.

LEVEL B   It's Monday, March the tenth.
He jumped from the van.
They ran to the castle.
They're drawing the sun and the stars.
There's a duck in this basket.

LEVEL C   The staff have lunch at one.
The farmer ran to his barn in alarm.
I dropped my hat in the mud.
Did he laugh much?

---

27   ə:, ʌ, ɑ: **and** ɔ: **as in** *bird, bud, barn* **and** *board*

Concerns: all

Problem: making ə: as in *bird* distinct from each of the following vowels: ʌ as in *bud*, ɑ: as in *barn* and ɔ: as in *board*.

Ear training

i. DISTINGUISHING ə: AND ʌ AS IN *bird* AND *bud*.

LEVEL A   Same/different practice:
shirt shut
Pick out the ə: words:
shirt   purple   girl   bus   kerb   plum   circle   nut   skirt   fur

LEVEL B   Pick out the ə: words:
bird   rough   hunt   burn   cut   were   hers   work   cup
worm   nurse

LEVEL C   Same/different practice:
bird bud   burn bun   turn ton   hurt hut

ii. DISTINGUISHING ɑ: AND ə: AS IN *cart/curt*.

PRACTICE 143

LEVEL A   Pick out the ɑ: words:
car   girl   yard   aunt   circle   first   bath   skirt   dark   scarf

LEVEL B   Same/different practice:
first fast   burn barn

LEVEL C   Same/different practice:
fur far   firm farm   heard hard

iii. DISTINGUISHING ə: AND ɔ: AS IN *curt/caught*.

PRACTICE 144

LEVEL A   Same/different practice:
shirt short   fur four

LEVEL B   Same/different practice:
work walk

LEVEL C   Same/different practice:
burn born   turn torn   curl call

Production
i. Practise words with ə: like *bird*. This vowel is formed more centrally than the others in this exercise, and it is long. Some learners may follow it with an r sound, particularly if they have been exposed to English spelling; but as many English accents do this too, there is no urgent need to correct it.

PRACTICE 145

LEVEL A   Practise saying:
purple   girl   kerb   circle   shirt   skirt   fur   furry   curly
first   third

Practise saying:

bird   thirsty   were   hers   burn   work   church   worm   nurse   hurt   surgery

LEVEL C   Practise saying:

bird   burn   turn   hurt   fur   firm   heard   were   earn   learn   dirty   germ   serve   term   word   curl

ii. Practise sets of words like *bird, bud, barn* and *board*, to contrast these four vowel sounds. (LEVEL C only)

PRACTICE 146

LEVEL C   Practise saying:

bird	*bud*	–	*board*
–	*cut*	*cart*	*caught*
shirt	*shut*	–	*short*
fur	–	*far*	*four*
burn	*bun*	*barn*	*born*
hurt	*hut*	*heart*	–
turn	*ton*	–	*torn*
third	*thud*	–	*thawed*

iii. Practise lists and word pairs contrasting *bird* with *bud*, *barn* and *board*. (LEVELS A and B only) Use the material in PRACTICES 142, 143 and 144 above.

iv. Practise in sentences.

PRACTICE 147

LEVEL A   Stop at the kerb.
This is a girl's scarf.
The purple bus is from London.
Please can I have four plums.
He wore a purple shirt.

LEVEL B   X I've hurt my arm.
Y What have you done?
X I've burned it.
Y How?
X On the oven door.
Y Is it very sore?
X Yes, it is.
Y You must be careful.

LEVEL C   X Have you heard about my aunt?
Y Your aunt? No. I hope it's something nice!
X Yes, it is this time. She's won four hundred pounds on the pools!

Y That's wonderful! Now she'll be able to buy a small car.

X I'm sure she won't pass her driving test.

---

28 ɑ:, ʌ **and** ɔ **as in** *heart*, *hut* **and** *hot*

Concerns: Indians and Pakistanis

Problem: making these sounds sufficiently distinct.

Ear training

i. DISTINGUISHING ɑ: AND ɔ IN LISTS AND WORD PAIRS LIKE *heart*/*hot*.

PRACTICE 148

LEVEL A Same/different practice:
last lost

Pick out the ɔ words:
lost soft past last hot sock arm collar aunt bath

LEVEL B Same/different practice:
barks box   clerk clock   calf cough

Pick out the ɔ words:
box dark last doctor cough past barks far top

LEVEL C Same/different practice:
heart hot   mark mock   dark dock   part pot   cart cot

ii. DISTINGUISHING ɑ: AND ʌ IN LISTS AND WORD PAIRS LIKE *heart*/*hut*.

Use the material in PRACTICE 137 above.

iii. DISTINGUISHING ʌ AND ɔ IN WORD LISTS AND PAIRS LIKE *hut*/*hot*.

PRACTICE 149

LEVEL A Same/different practice:
colour collar   nut not

LEVEL B Same/different practice:
dog dug

Pick out the ɔ words:
lot dog rough hunt tongue cut top jump cup doctor stop hot

LEVEL C Same/different practice:
cot cut   hot hut   shot shut   model muddle

130

Production

i. Practise ɑ: as in *cart*. Use the material in PRACTICE 139 above.

ii. Practise ʌ as in *cut*. Use the material in PRACTICE 140 above.

iii. Practise ɔ as in *cot*.

PRACTICE 150

LEVEL A   Practise saying:
*not   hot   sock   box   stop   collar   hop   hopping   lollipop
lost   cotton*

LEVEL B   Practise saying:
dog   top   lot   stop   got   clock   cough   doctor   wrong

LEVEL C   Practise saying:
*boss   dock   shot   watch   hot   lock   not   fog   job   college
box*

iv. Practise contrasting ɑ: and ɔ as in *cart/cot*. Use the material in PRACTICE 148 above.

v. Practise contrasting ɑ: and ʌ as in *cart/cut*. Use the material in PRACTICE 137 above.

vi. Practise contrasting ʌ and ɔ as in *cut/cot*. Use the material in PRACTICE 149 above.

vii. Practise them in sentences.

PRACTICE 151

LEVEL A   X I've lost my scarf.
Y What colour is it?
X It's dark green.
Y Is it made of cotton?
X Cotton! No, it's very warm. It's made of wool.

LEVEL B   X I must go to the doctor.
Y What's wrong?
X I've got a bad cough.
Y Go this afternoon.
X Yes. The surgery's at half past one.

LEVEL C   They laughed at the duck on the bus.
Come and watch television.
The large box is locked.
Park your car in the staff car park.
The boss shut the cupboard door.

29   i **and** i: **as in** bit **and** beat

Concerns: Indians, Pakistanis, Greek and Italian speakers

Problem: making these sound distinct. Failure to make i: as in beat long enough is often largely to blame for confusion, but the two vowels also need slightly different mouth positions. The front of the tongue should be higher for i: than for i. i is a much more 'relaxed' sound.

Ear training

DISTINGUISHING i AND i: IN LISTS AND PAIRS LIKE bit/beat.

PRACTICE 152

LEVEL A   Same/different practice:
it eat

Pick out the i: words:
*feet   sink   inch   green   with   this   these   three   each   tea
bit*

LEVEL B   Same/different practice:
sit seat   live leave

LEVEL C   Same/different practice:
bit beat   grin green   ship sheep   live leave   lid lead

Production

i. Practise i words like *bit*. Use the material in PRACTICE 138 above.

ii. Practise i: words.

PRACTICE 153

LEVEL A   Practise saying:
*feet   green   three   these   each   tea   knee   see   sweep
street*

LEVEL B   Practise saying:
*seat   leave   sheep   leaf   week   cheap   teeth   beach   street
peaches   police   three*

LEVEL C   Practise saying:
*beat   green   sheep   leave   reach   heat   read   seen   meat
these   speak   three   each*

iii. Practise i and i: in contrast. Use the material in PRACTICE 152 above.

iv. Practise these in sentences.

132

LEVEL A This is his cup of tea, not mine.
They're sixpence each.
Mrs. Green's sweeping the kitchen.
Have you got a threepenny bit?
Tony lives in King Street.

LEVEL B She's sitting on the beach.
I live in Ship Street.
Tony's leaving King Street.
These peaches are very cheap.
This week there's a film about the police.
There are three sheep on a little hill.

LEVEL C The ship is leaving this morning.
There are lots of sheep on these hills.
This is Mr. Flynn speaking.
These are three shillings each.
Make a list of the things you've seen on the beach today.

---

30 ɔ **and** ɔ: **as in** *not* **and** *naught*

Concerns: all

Problem: making these distinct. Length is the first difference to work on.

Ear training

DISTINGUISHING ɔ AND ɔ: IN LISTS AND WORD PAIRS LIKE *not/naught*.

PRACTICE 155

LEVEL A Pick out the ɔ: words:
four box walk not fork stop hot sock your bought

LEVEL B Pick out the ɔ: words:
draw lot top small tall got sore clock cough paw

LEVEL C Same/different practice:
not naught pot port shot short

Production

i. Practise ɔ words, like *cot*. Use the material in PRACTICE 150 above.

ii. Practise ɔ: words.

PRACTICE 156

LEVEL A   Practise saying:
four walk fork your bought ball door small stall
saw warm tall wore hall drawing

LEVEL B   Practise saying:
draw small tall sore paw claw drawn North more
fall roar horse forty walked quarter tortoise four

LEVEL C   Practise saying:
naught port short all law floor caught ought
talk morning sort born sports thought court door

iii. Practise this contrast. Use the material in PRACTICE 155 above.

iv. Practise these in sentences.

PRACTICE 157

LEVEL A   I bought a ball.
It's hot.
Can I have a lollipop please?
Are these your football socks?
What are you drawing?
I'm drawing a market stall and a dog.

LEVEL B   You've got a bad cough. See the doctor.
It's quarter to four.
The dog's got the ball.
Here are a lot of horses.
They walked forty miles.

LEVEL C   The boss has lost his watch.
She talked and talked. All the morning!
You ought to lock the office door.
What sort of sport do you watch?
I'm not sure if I like it at all.
Their ship is in dock at Portsmouth.

---

31   u **and** u: **as in** *look* **and** *Luke*

Concerns: Indians, Pakistanis, Greek and Italian speakers

Problem: making these distinct. Length is an important difference here.

Ear training

DISTINGUISHING u AND u: IN PAIRS AND WORD LISTS.

134

LEVEL A   Pick out the u: words:
shoe who book hook good blue two put spoon ruler new

LEVEL B   Pick out the u: words:
moon move too full stood through wood food bull moo fruit

LEVEL C   Same/different practice:
pulls pools   full fool

Pick out the u: words:
boot would shook tool loot screw use could should loose

Production

i. Practise u words.

PRACTICE 159

LEVEL A   Practise saying:
book hook good put foot wool cook look

LEVEL B   Practise saying:
full stood wood bull took looked cooked

LEVEL C   Practise saying:
pull full hood hook shook would could should look

ii. Practise u: words.

PRACTICE 160

LEVEL A   Practise saying:
shoe blue two spoon ruler new smooth who

LEVEL B   Practise saying:
moon move too through food fruit

LEVEL C   Practise saying:
pool fool who whose Luke boot tool loot screw use soon tune

iii. Practise in sentences.

PRACTICE 161

LEVEL A   Who's this?
Look at the blue books.
Can I have a new ruler please?
Put the spoons on the table please.
Who's got new shoes?

(N.B. Make sure you do *not* stress the unstressed syllables where u should be used. These are the words shown in brackets.)
There was a full moon.
We must move this food.
It's ten to two. (to)
This bottle is too full.
The bull looked at the farmer, but it didn't move.
They're going to the moon. (to)

LEVEL C Fools and their money are soon parted.
Look before you leap. (you)
You should use the proper tools. (you, should)
Who'd have thought it?
He shook with laughter from head to toe. (to)
You would go if you could. (you, you)

---

32 ə: and ə as in *murder*: ə: first syllable, and ə second.

Concerns: all

Problem: making these sounds distinct, and making use of the weak, neutrally-formed vowel, ə. See the notes on page 15 about ə; the occurrence of this vowel is closely connected with rhythm; it occurs frequently in unstressed syllables. These may be monosyllabic structural words like *of* or the unstressed minor syllables of words like fa*ther*. It never occurs stressed. Both ə and ə: are formed centrally in the mouth; ə: is long, and ə is always very short and weak.

Ear training

i. IDENTIFYING ə: IN WORD LISTS.

PRACTICE 162

LEVEL A Pick out the ə: words:
thirty ruler number furry shoulder banana jersey shirt sweater leather curly

LEVEL B Pick out the ə: words:
thirsty ladder first smaller doctor about stomach hurt early supper along summer

LEVEL C Pick out the ə: words:
earnings perhaps surprised longer firm working future abroad personal machine perfect motor service remember

136

ii. Let the children identify the rhythmic shape of the words in PRACTICE 162 above: ☐ ❑ or ☐ or ❑ ☐ or ❑ ❑ ☐ or ❑ ☐ ❑ .

Production

i. Practise ə words, noticing the rhythmic shape of each one. Remember that the ə syllable must be very weak in contrast to the stressed one. The ə syllables are shown in **bold** italic.

PRACTICE 163

LEVEL A   Practise saying:
ruler   number   shoulder   sweater   leather   over   under
grocer   banana   yesterday   altogether

LEVEL B   Practise saying:
ladder   doctor   summer   smaller   bigger   longer
stomach   paraffin   about   alight

LEVEL C   Practise saying:
longer   greater   faster   future   motor   method   perhaps
surprised   remember   machine   saturday   November   seasons
suppose   afford

ii. Practise ə: words like *shirt*. Use the material in PRACTICE 145 above.

iii. Practise these in sentences, paying particular attention to rhythm. The exact sound of ə is not important, but it must be short and unobtrusive. ə syllables are marked.

PRACTICE 164

LEVEL A   x What's thé time?
           y It's sevén thirty.
           x Thé clock on thé wall is wrong.
           y It wás fast yestérday.

LEVEL B   x Hallo. You're early.
           y Yes. We finished work early tóday. What's thé time?
           x Quartér past six. Was thé bus very full?
           y No, bút it wás hot; ánd now I 'm very thirsty.
           x Come ánd sit down. Here's á cup óf tea.

LEVEL C   x Which firm do you work for?
           y Palmérs ánd Masón.
           x They make furnitúre, don't they?
           y Yes, that's right. A lot óf it is exported.

137

Diphthongs (see page 12)

33.1   ei **as in** *late*

Concerns: all

Problem: making a clear diphthong. Indians and Pakistanis will confuse words like *late* and *let*, making ei sound too much like e.

Ear training

DISTINGUISHING ei AND e IN PAIRS LIKE *late*/*let* AND IN LISTS.

PRACTICE 165

LEVEL A   Pick out the ei words:
eight   pen   wet   *gate*   men   *straight*   *scales*   *dates*   *grapes*
eggs   red   *table*   *raining*   went   *playing*

LEVEL B   Same/different practice:
late let   gate get

LEVEL C   Same/different practice:
pain pen   eight ate   wait wet   main men   tale tell

Production

i. Practise ei words.

PRACTICE 166

LEVEL A   Practise saying:
*eight   gate   scales   dates   straight   grapes   table   may
plane   raining   play   train   day*

LEVEL B   Practise saying:
*late   gate   made   radio   flame   lake   came   same   eighty
ache   say   take   painting*

LEVEL C   Practise saying:
*pain   eight   wait   main   name   afraid   explain   able   crane
drain   complain   late   newspapers   say*

ii. Practise e words, like *let*. Use the material in PRACTICE 131 above.

iii. Practise word pairs and lists to contrast ei and e as in *late*/*let*. Use the material in PRACTICE 165 above.

138

LEVEL A Can I have some grapes please?
Is this a red train?
Here's a plane from India.
It was raining on Wednesday.
It was a very wet day.
Eight men are sitting at the table.

LEVEL B He's listening to the radio.
She's painting a picture of a lake.
They have eighty hens in the shed.
These letters are the same.
I came to England eight years ago.

LEVEL C What's her name?
I'm afraid I'm late.
What do the newspapers say? Have you read them?
Please wait while I explain something to Mr. Henson.
Can you tell me why they're complaining?

33.2 ou **as in** *no*

Concerns: all

Problem: making this sound a clear diphthong and not too much
like ɔ as in *not* or ɔ: as in *naught*.

Ear training

i. DISTINGUISHING ou AND ɔ: AS IN *note/naught* IN LISTS AND WORD
PAIRS.

PRACTICE 168

LEVEL A Same/different practice:
boat bought

Pick out the ou words:
coat four hall home toe nose door fork old

LEVEL B Same/different practice:
foal fall

Pick out the ou words:
*coal drawn slow oats goat horse smoke comb short
post*

LEVEL C Same/different practice:
coat court no nor coal call note naught

ii. DISTINGUISHING ou AND ɔ AS IN *note/not* IN LISTS AND WORD PAIRS.

PRACTICE 169

LEVEL A   Pick out the ou words:
coat   snow   old   hot   cold   home   hop   box   boat

LEVEL B   Same/different practice:
goat got

Pick out the ou words:
*comb   cold   smoke   cough   coal   top   dog   goat   oats
spot   post   slow*

LEVEL C   Same/different practice:
hope hop   note not

Production

i. Practise ou words.

PRACTICE 170

LEVEL A   Practise saying:
coat   boat   home   snow   old   nose   toe   road

LEVEL B   Practise saying:
comb   cold   smoke   coat   goat   oats   post   slow   ago   coal

LEVEL C   Practise saying:
coat   no   coal   note   hope   phone   go   so   nobody

ii. Practise ɔ words like *not*. Use the material in PRACTICE 150 above.

iii. Practise ɔː words like *naught*. Use the material in PRACTICE 156 above.

iv. Practise ou and ɔː words in contrast, like *no/nor*. Use the material in PRACTICE 168 above.

v. Practise ou and ɔ words in contrast, like *note/not*. Use the material in PRACTICE 169 above.

vi. Practise in sentences.

PRACTICE 171

LEVEL A   Tony bought a boat.
This is very hot.
Who's got the old box?
My nose is cold.
There is snow in the road.

140

LEVEL B The horse is eating its oats.
I've drawn a postman.
We came to England four years ago.
Do you like coal fires?
You're very slow. What's wrong?

LEVEL C They took their complaint to a court of law.
Here's a note from Tony.
It's not from Tony. It's from John.
This is not your coat, is it?
Nobody answered the phone, so we thought you were all out.

33.3   au **as in** *now*

Concerns: Turkish and Italian speakers. Some Indians and
Pakistanis

Problem: making this into a real diphthong and distinguishing
it clearly from ou as in *no*.

Ear training

DISTINGUISHING au FROM ou, AS IN *now/no*.

PRACTICE 172

LEVEL A Pick out the au words:
brown **out** *down* road comb *ground* cl*ou*d snow
m*ou*th old

LEVEL B Same/different practice:
found phoned   now no

LEVEL C Same/different practice:
Slough slow   row row   town tone

Production

i. Practise au words.

PRACTICE 173

LEVEL A Practise saying:
brown   out   down   ground   cloud   mouth   how   now

LEVEL B Practise saying:
*found   now   shout   South   house   pouch   cow   counter
mouse   brown*

Practise saying:
slough   row   town   sound   round   allow   proud   noun
pound   frowned   South

ii. Practise ou words, like *no*. Use the material in
PRACTICE 170 above.

iii. Practise in sentences.

PRACTICE 174

LEVEL A   How much is the brown comb?
He's outside in the playground.
Sit down now.
The ground is very rough.
Is that black cloud coming?

LEVEL B   There's a brown cow outside.
I've found a mouse under the counter.
He phoned Mr. South.
Is this our house? No, it isn't.
Don't shout.

LEVEL C   Slough is a town in the South.
What a row they're making!
Now stand in a row, and don't make a sound.
We're proud of our town.
He turned round slowly and frowned.

33.4   ai **as in** *buy* **and** ɔi **as in** *boy*

Concerns: all, except for some Indians and Pakistanis who are
familiar with ai as in *buy*; Italians and Greeks will be able to
learn ɔi as in *boy* fairly easily

Problem: making these sounds clear diphthongs.

Ear training

IDENTIFYING ai WORDS LIKE *nine*.

PRACTICE 175

LEVEL A   Pick out the ai words:
nine   no   number   nut   night   nine   man   mine   money
boy   buy   bunch   pint

LEVEL B   Pick out the ai words:
night   nut   not   ninety   slide   shine   sign   sun   sound
towns   times   tons   fly

142

Pick out the ai words:

file *mile* *line* but bout bite fun *fine* foil *tile* told
sky *high*

Production

i. Practise words with ai like *buy.*

PRACTICE 176

LEVEL A Practise saying:
buy *nine* *five* *nine* *I'm* *right* *sky* *pint* *like* *tie* *eye*

LEVEL B Practise saying:
pint *slide* *night* *fly* *fight* *shine* *light* *times* *sign* *why*
five

LEVEL C Practise saying:
tie *file* *tile* *mile* *high* *die* *cry* *sky* *fry* bite *fine*

Ear training

IDENTIFYING ɔi WORDS LIKE *boy.* (LEVELS B and C only)

PRACTICE 177

LEVEL B Pick out the ɔi words:
join **point** pint port pound **poi**son all **oil** born **boy**
buy.

LEVEL C Pick out the ɔi words:
toy **toil** tall tale tool *taller* **toils** en**joy** ball bull
boil fall **foil** foul an**noy** **roy**al im*plore* plough em**ploy.**

Production

i. Practise ɔi words. (LEVELS B and C only)

PRACTICE 178

LEVEL B Practise saying:
boy *point* *join* *oil* *poison*

LEVEL C Practise saying:
toy *foil* *royal* *boil* *soil* *enjoy* *employ* *annoy* *boy*

ii. Practise in sentences.

PRACTICE 179

LEVEL A I'm buying a tie.
This boy is nine.
Would you like five pints or six?
Look right, look left, look right again.

A pint of oil please.
Five pints of oil please.
Point to the sign.
Why are you fighting?
Join these pieces with glue.

LEVEL C Wrap the meat in foil.
File these papers please.
Here's a toy for the little boy.
They employ nine boys in the tile works.

33.5 Diphthongs ending with ə – iə as in *here* **ɛə as in** *hair*

Concerns: all

Problem: general difficulty in saying these as clear diphthongs.
A final r sound may be added by some speakers, but this does
not matter too much as long as it is not too prominent.

Ear training

Make the children listen very carefully to iə words and beat
or identify the rhythms.

PRACTICE 180

LEVEL A Listen and identify or beat the rhythms:
here   ear

LEVEL B Listen and beat or identify the rhythms:
dear   near   we're

LEVEL C Listen and identify or beat the rhythms:
hear   fear   gear   beer   we're

Production

Practise iə as in *here*. If necessary practise i as in *bit*, and then
tail that vowel sound off into the neutral vowel ə, all
within one syllable beat. Use the material in PRACTICE 180
above.

Ear training

Make the children listen very carefully to ɛə words and beat
or identify the rhythms of the practice words.

PRACTICE 181

LEVEL A Listen and identify or beat the rhythms:
where   there   wearing   stairs   square

144

Listen and identify or beat the rhythms:
fare hair careful chair

Listen and identify or beat the rhythms:
share dare care pear fair tear prayer

Production

i. Practise ɛə as in *hair*. If necessary practise e as in *let*, and then tailing that vowel sound off into the neutral vowel ə, but all within the space of one syllable beat. Use the material in PRACTICE 181 above.

ii. Practise in sentences.

PRACTICE 182

LEVEL A   Here's Tony.
Where's Carol?
They're sixpence each.
What are you wearing?
This is my ear.
There's a box upstairs.
This is a square yard.

LEVEL B   This dress is very dear.
This year we're in class 3.
Christmas is very near.
Half fare please.
She's got dark hair.
Be careful! That chair is broken!

LEVEL C   Share this.
Do you dare?
I don't care.
We're coming to the meeting here tonight.
I can't hear him very clearly.
Change gear at the bottom of the hill.
Would you like a pear?
The decision isn't fair.
Do you like beer?
I fear you're right.
Don't tear that paper up.

34   Triphthongs, or the two-syllable alternatives: as in *player,*
spire, lawyer, hour **and** *mower*: (See page 13.)

Concerns: all

Problem: fitting the vowel into one syllable beat, or producing
the diphthong plus the neutral vowel version which occupies
two syllables: e.g. ˈplei – jə (*pla – yer*). The latter will
probably be easier for most learners.

Ear training

Get the children to pick out the different triphthong vowels
from the following list, taking each triphthong in turn. Also let
them identify the rhythms. (LEVEL C only)

PRACTICE 183

LEVEL C   Pick out the different vowels, taking each in turn. Identify
the rhythms:
flower hour shower   player   spire fire   lawyer   mower lower

Production

i. Practice these words. Use the material in PRACTICE 183
above, (LEVEL C only)

ii. Practise in sentences. (LEVEL C only)

PRACTICE 184

LEVEL C   She was selling flowers.
It took an hour.
We had a few showers of rain.
He's a good football player.
The church has a beautiful spire.
Let's turn down the fire.
We must ask a lawyer.
We need a mower for this grass.
Let's lower the flag now.

---

35   Long vowels at the end of words, as in *knee*

Concerns: Italians

Problem: making these vowels long enough. The long vowels
are the iː as in *knee*, ɑː as in *far*, ɔː as in *four*, əː as in *fur* and
uː as in *shoe*. This applies also to diphthongs.

Ear training

Beat the rhythms of these sentences, to establish where the stresses come.

PRACTICE 185

LEVEL A   A bar of soap is in the bathroom.
I saw a car outside the house.
A boy is in the tree.
The sky is blue today.
I've hurt my knee.

LEVEL B   I've got a sore knee.
She's making the tea.
What did she say?
Where is the glue?

LEVEL C   Is it very far?
I'm going to a play.
They'll go by air.
What's the pay?
I don't agree.
Three.more.
They employ a few women.
You should insure this.
They enjoy music.

Production

i. Practise the following words, giving due length to the vowel, and in the two-syllable words to the stressed vowel.

PRACTICE 186

LEVEL A   Practise saying:
*bar   blue   car   boy   no   tree   sky   snow   pea   saw   buy
two   three   four   eye*

LEVEL B   Practise saying:
day   sore   tea   sea   knee   glue   show   fly   cow   high   say

LEVEL C   Practise saying:
*far   now   play   air   pay   few   more   employ   agree
career   enjoy   insure*

ii. Practise saying the sentences in PRACTICE 185 above.

3 Rhythm Exercises

(See page 23 on the rhythm of English and page 32 on techniques for practising it.)

1 Simple rhythms to beat

2 Sentence rhythms to beat

Introduce these, one at a time, as rhythms to beat. Then show
the children sentences which match. Later on you will be able
to say a sentence to them and let them identify or beat the
rhythm straight away.

1 ⬜⬜

Dah dah

What's this?   Good-bye.
Yes, please.   Stand up.
By plane.   They're books.

2 ⬜ ▭ ⬜

Dah di dah

What's your name?
Two and six.
Sixpence each.
Yes, I have.
They're the same.
Here's your coat.
What's the time?

3 ⬜ ▭ ⬜ ▭

Dah di dah di

What's he wearing?
No, he isn't.
Three and seven.
Tony's ruler.
I'm from Cyprus.
There's a bus stop.
Half past seven.
Green and yellow.

4 ▭ ⬜ ▭ ⬜ ▭

Di dah di dah di

Because it's raining.
I've lost my pencil.
I've spilt the water.
He lives in King Street.
Is this November?

5 ▭ ⬜ ▭ ▭ ⬜

Di dah di di dah

She's buying some eggs.
He's wearing a hat.
It's quarter to three.
They're under the chair.

3 Sentences to practise weak forms and neutral vowel

Beat the rhythms of the following sentences, as in the last exercise, and/or identify them from sets of squares. Pay particular attention to the weak syllables, making sure they do not get stressed or 'over-pronounced'. They can fade well into the background. Then practise saying the sentences, using the vowels ə, u and i, as in (*moth*)*er*, *put* and *bit* respectively. where possible. See page 11.

1 She's *ma*king a *dress*.
vowels: *She's* (i), *a* (ə)

2 He's *ea*ting an *egg*.
vowels: *He's* (i), *an* (ə)

3 *What* are you *do*ing?
vowels: *are* (ə), *you* (u)

4 *Where* do they *live*?
vowels: *do* (u)

5 *He's* from *In*dia.
vowels: *from* (ə)

6 It's for *To*ny.
vowels: *for* (ə)

7 I'm *go*ing to *school*.
vowels: *to* (u) or (ə)

8 *What's* the *time*?
vowels: *the* (ə)

9 It's *red* and *green*.
vowels: *and* (ə)

10   I can *jump three* feet.   ▫ ▫ ☐ ☐ ▫
     vowels: *can* (ə)

11   We *went* to the *mar*ket.   ▫ ☐ ▫ ▫ ☐ ▫
     vowels: *We* (i), *to* (u), *the* (ə)

12   I'd *like* some *milk* please.   ▫ ☐ ▫ ☐ ▫
     vowels: *some* (ə)

13   *Where* are the *app*les?   ☐ ▫ ▫ ☐ ▫
     vowels: *are* (ə), *the* (i)

---

4   Rhymes and songs

1. What am I doing?   Tune: Here we come gathering nuts in May. (Refer to *Scope*, Stage 1 record of Songs)

Sing with appropriate actions. Further verses can be invented by substituting new lines for *I'm washing my hands*.

What am I doing?
I'm washing my hands,
Washing my hands,
Washing my hands.
What am I doing?
I'm washing my hands,
Early in the morning.

2. Here comes a big red bus   Tune: The Muffin Man. (Refer to record)

Substitute a local name for *London town* e.g. *Bradford town*, *Birmingham*, etc.

Here comes a big red bus,
A big red bus, a big red bus.
Here comes a big red bus
To go to London town.

3. Fruit and vegetables

Practise the first three lines of this rhyme with the class as a whole. Then split the class into groups, so that each group can take a line. Repeat, letting individuals take a line. Try practising it very quietly at the beginning, and getting louder and louder. Make sure the nouns are stressed in the right place.

Oranges and lemons
Onions and garlic
Cabbages and peas,

Bananas and apples
Potatoes and carrots
Tomatoes and grapes.

4. Where are my pencils?   Tune: Refer to record

Where are my pencils?
Where, oh, where?
Are they in the cupboard?
Are they on a chair?
Ho ho de ho, diddle diddle dee,
Here are my pencils,
One, two, three.

5. Heads and shoulders   Tune: Refer to record

Sing or say this, with appropriate actions.

Heads and shoulders, knees and toes,
Knees and toes, knees and toes,
Heads and shoulders, knees and toes,
We all go round together.
Eyes and ears, and mouth and nose,
Mouth and nose, mouth and nose,
Eyes and ears and mouth and nose,
We all go round together.

6. I'm wearing a shirt

This rhyme should be said so as to sound like a train slowly pulling out of a station and then gathering speed.
I'm *wea*ring a *shirt*, *shirt*, *shirt*, *shirt*,
A *jer*sey, *jer*sey, *jer*sey, *jer*sey,
A *hat* 'n coat, *hat* 'n coat, *hat* 'n coat, *hat* 'n coat,
A *car*digan, a *car*digan, a *car*digan, a *car*digan.

152

7. There's a bedroom   Tune: Refer to record

There's a bedroom
And a bathroom
And a kitchen
And a living room,
And a garden with some flowers
Where I like to play.

There's a bedroom
And a bathroom
And a kitchen
And a living room
And a garden where I work
On a nice sunny day.

8. Longer and longer

Build up the following sequences rhythmically and chorally.

A *bird*
A *bird* in a *tree*
A *bird* in a *tree* in the *park*

A *squ*irrel
A *squ*irrel on a *see*saw
A *squ*irrel on a *see*saw in the *play*ground.

*Wel*lingtons
*Wel*lingtons, an um*bre*lla
*Wel*lingtons, an um*bre*lla and a *rain*hat.

9. The moon   W. Kingdon Ward

Oh! Look at the moon
Like a big silver spoon
So round and so bright
In the sky
In the night.

10. This and that   R. Bennet

I like this one,
I like that.
This is thin
And that is fat.

F

I like thin things,
I like fat
I like this one,
I like that.

11. Water in bottles   R. Bennet

Water in bottles,
Water in pans,
Water in kettles,
Water in cans.
It's always the shape
Of whatever it's in,
Bucket or kettle,
Or bottle or tin.

12. An apple a day   Proverb

An apple a day
Keeps the doctor away.

13. Early to bed   Proverb

Early to bed,
Early to rise,
Makes you healthy,
Wealthy and wise.

14. The Grand old Duke of York   (Traditional)

Oh, the grand old Duke of York,
He had ten thousand men,
He marched them up to the top of the hill,
And he marched them down again.

And when they were up, they were up,
And when they were down they were down,
And when they were only halfway up
They were neither up nor down.

15. The animals went in two by two   (Refer to record)

The animals went in two by two,
    hurrah, hurrah!
The animals went in two by two,
    hurrah, hurrah!

The animals went in two by two,
The elephant and the kangaroo,
And they all went into the ark,
Just to get out of the rain.
  (Each verse, repeat as above)
The animals went in three by three,
The wasp, the ant, and the bumble bee.

The animals went in four by four,
The big hippopotamus stuck in the door.

The animals went in five by five,
By eating all day they kept alive.

(Three or four verses of this song are probably enough. For
full text see *Time for a Song*, Lee and Dodderidge,
Longman, 1963.)

16. A Spider   W. Kingdon-Ward

I saw a spider
Crawl – crawl – crawl
I saw a spider
Crawling up the wall.

17. Clocks

The town hall clock goes tick, tock, tick, tock,
The clock on the shelf goes tick tock, tick tock, tick tock,
   tick tock,
My little watch goes ticker tacker, ticker tacker, ticker tacker,
   tick.

18. Oats, beans and barley   (Refer to record)

The farmer sows his seed,
The farmer sows his seed,
Oats, beans and barley, O!
The farmer sows his seed.

The wind begins to blow,
(etc)

The rain begins to fall
The sun begins to shine
The seed begins to grow
The farmer cuts his grain

The farmer binds the sheaves
And now the harvest's in.

19. A dog and a horse

(Particularly for word stress)

A *dog* and a *hor*se, a *shee*p and a *cow*,
A *don*key, a *ti*ger, a *mon*key, a *li*on,
An *el*ephant, a *cro*codile, a *but*terfly, a *kan*garoo,
And – a *ca*terpillar, *ca*terpillar, *ca*terpillar, *ca*terpillar.

20. What do they say?

What does the cat say? Miau! miau!
What does the dog say? Bow! – bow!
What does the donkey say? Hee! – haw!
What does the crow say? Caw! – caw!
What does the farmer say? Shoo! – shoo!
What does the cow say? Moo! – moo!
And what do they all say?
(All together . . . . .)

21. I sent a letter to my love   (Refer to record)

When you have taught the song, play the traditional game that
goes with it.

I sent a letter to my love
And on the way I dropped it,
One of you has picked it up
And put it in his pocket.

22. What are you going to be?   Paul Edmonds

What are you going to be?
What are you going to be?
I shall be a policeman
That's the life for me

What are you going to be?
What are you going to be?
I shall be a soldier
That's the life for me

(Let the children suggest other careers for themselves, in
line 3.)

156

23. Ernest was an elephant   A. A. Milne

Ernest was an elephant, a great big fellow,
Leonard was a lion with a six-foot tail,
George was a goat, and his beard was yellow,
And James was a very small snail.

Bibliography

AUSTRALIA COMMONWEALTH OFFICE OF EDUCATION 'The Italian Student', and 'The Greek Student', *English as a New Language: a bulletin for teachers of new Australians*, Vol. 3, No. 4, January 1953, and Vol. 8, No. 4, March 1962.

CANDLIN, C. 'Pronunciation Problems of Asian Immigrants', *English for Immigrants*, the journal of the Associations of Teachers for the Education of Pupils from Overseas, Vol. 2, No. 2, Spring 1969.

DAKIN, J. *Songs and Rhymes for the Teaching of English*, Pupils' book and Teacher's book, Longman, 1968.

DERRICK, J. *Teaching English to Immigrants*, Longman, 1966.

GIMSON, A. C. *An Introduction to the Pronunciation of English*, Arnold, 1962.

HARLEY, A. H. 'The Pronunciation of Urdu' introduction to T. G. BAILEY *Teach Yourself Urdu*, English Universities Press.

JAMES, A. G. 'Stories from the Punjab', *English for Immigrants*, the journal of the Associations of Teachers for the Education of Pupils from Overseas, Vol. 2, No. 2, Spring 1969.

JONES, D. *The Pronunciation of English*, Cambridge University Press, 4th edition, 1956.

JONES, D. *An English Pronouncing Dictionary*, J. M. Dent & Sons Ltd. 13th edition 1967.

LEE, W. R. AND DODDERIDGE, M. *Time for a Song*, Longman, 1963.

LEE, W. R. AND KOULLIS, L. *Argonauts' English Course*, Oxford University Press, 1966.

MACCARTHY, P. A. D. *English Pronunciation*, Heffer, 4th edition, 1956.

MISRA, B. G., AND FAIRBANKS, G. *Spoken and Written Hindi*, Cornell University Press, 1965.

O'CONNOR, J. D. *Better English Pronunciation*, Cambridge University Press, 1967.

PRING, J. *Colloquial English Pronunciation*, Longman, 1959.

The following unpublished reports and dissertations are available for reference at the Centre for Information on Language Teaching, State House, High Holborn, London, W.C.1.:

BANSAL, R. K. *The Intelligibility of Indian English*, London University Ph. D. Thesis, 1966.

HARRY, P. *A Study of Spoken Gujerati in its relation to the teaching of English to Gujerati learners*, Edinburgh University diploma dissertation, 1962.

PERREN, G. E. *The Construction and Application of Some Experimental Tests of English Ability for Overseas Students in Britain*: a synoptic report of some research at Manchester University, 1958/60.

Also but not available at C.I.L.T.

GREEN, G. *Some Problems of English Language Learning in Cyprus*, Leeds University diploma dissertation, 1962.

Index

Individual sounds are listed at the end of the alphabetical index and named by their phonetic symbols. The order is that of the lists on the inside of the front and back covers of the book.

ɔi (b*oy*)   12, 14; problems 142 (all)

iə (b*eer*)   12; problems 144 (all)

ɛə (b*ear*)   12; problems 144 (all);
regional variation 17

uə (t*our*)   12, 14; variations 17

ɔə (d*oor*)   12; variations 17

eu (ou used in this book) 10(fn)

a   (in northern England) 17